The
DENSITY
of the
PRESENT

The
DENSITY
of the
PRESENT

Selected Writings

Gustavo
Gutiérrez

ORBIS BOOKS

Maryknoll, New York 10545

The Catholic Foreign Mission Society of America (Maryknoll) recruits and trains people for overseas missionary service. Through Orbis Books, Maryknoll aims to foster the international dialogue that is essential to mission. The books published, however, reflect the opinions of their authors and are not meant to represent the official position of the society. To obtain more information about Maryknoll or Orbis Books, please visit our website at www.maryknoll.org.

Library of Congress Cataloging-in-Publication Data
Gutiérrez, Gustavo, 1928–
   [Densidad del presente. English]
   The density of the present : selected writings / Gustavo Gutiérrez.
     p. cm.
   Includes bibliographical references and index.
   ISBN 1-57075-246-X (pbk.)
   1. Liberation theology. 2. Catholic Church — Doctrines.
I. Title.
BT83.57.G85413 1999
230.2–dc21   93-35645

To
María Agustina Rivas
and Irene McCormack
and to those like them
who daily and with simplicity
have given and continue to give their lives.
Their testimony reminds us
of the evangelical density
of our present.

Contents

Part Three
SPIRITUALITY AND THEOLOGY

PART ONE

Social Teaching and the Option for the Poor

Without doubt John Paul II has given a decisive impulse to the social teachings of the Church. In the direction initiated by John XXIII and Paul VI he has introduced new themes and perspectives. He has extended the opening to "new things" (rerum novarum) *to the international dimension of poverty and injustice, as well as to the social and economic structures that produce them. All this has reinforced the ethical character of a teaching that effects an evangelical discernment through the vagaries of human history.*

One of his great contributions is the way he reads this teaching from the perspective of the preferential option for the poor, for the other (the others) of a rich society which tends to consider itself self-sufficient. This focus is rich in promise, reminding us of the central role of the human person in the construction of a just society. At the same time it recovers the biblical roots that give depth to the quest for justice, bound indissolubly to the quest for the reign of God (see Matt. 6:33).

– 1 –

The Gospel of Work
Reflections on *Laborem Exercens*

The purpose of these pages, especially the first and last sections, is to present the theological aspects of the encyclical *Laborem Exercens* (LE). But the theological perspective makes up the framework of the whole text. Throughout the encyclical there are explicit references to reflection on the faith. One seldom finds such strong biblical and theological content in documents dealing with social issues.

Although we intend to focus on *Laborem Exercens,* it is also necessary to refer to other texts of John Paul II, especially his two previous encyclicals, because of their important place in papal teaching. A detailed analysis would show a deep continuity between those documents and *Laborem Exercens.* We shall not make such an analysis here, but a few references will make the point.

This is a dense — sometimes repetitious — and fully developed text, which perhaps does not reveal all its richness on a first reading. But its basic outline and central ideas are clear. In these pages we would like to assist in that reading from the viewpoint of theological reflection. By using numerous citations, we hope to make the text speak for itself.

The novel expression "Gospel of work," and its derivations, are clearly central to the theological bases of the encyclical. But to measure its depth we should first analyze the type of reflection on faith that we find in the document. Then we must assess its

Paper presented at the first Hugo Echegaray University Seminar, organized by UNEC, published in G. Gutiérrez, R. Ames, J. Iguiñiz, and C. Chipoco, *Sobre el trabajo humano: Comentarios a la Encíclica "Laborem Exercens"* (Lima: CEP, 1982).

call to a commitment by the whole Church to the world of work. All these considerations will lead to clues about how to live the Christian faith in that context.

A Theological Style

We must pay attention to the style of theological reflection used in the encyclical, in order to grasp the meaning of some of the affirmations it makes.

Discerning the Signs of the Times

From his first encyclical, *Redemptor Hominis* (RH), John Paul II pointed out that "John XXIII and Paul VI represent a stage, which I would describe as a threshold, from which I want...to move into the future" (RH 2). In his second encyclical, *Dives in Misericordia* (DM), he affirmed: "in the present phase of the history of the Church we propose as a preeminent task to put into action the doctrine of the great Council" (DM 1). This stage in the life of the Church, marked by the Council, opened new perspectives which cannot now be closed off. Great conciliar themes are thus introduced in John Paul's teaching in his effort to "put into action the doctrine" of Vatican II.

One of the expressions that helped to shape the conciliar spirit was introduced by John XXIII when he made it a task of the Church, and in particular of the Council, to learn to discern "the signs of the times." The expression is deeply rooted in Scripture (see Matt. 16:3) and assumes that historical events are a challenge and an enrichment for the Christian faith. Vatican II, especially in the constitution "The Church in the World,"[1] echoed this concern of John XXIII. Paul VI vigorously took up this perspective in *Populorum Progressio* and in *Octogesima Adveniens*.

John Paul II was already following the Council's line when he wrote in *Redemptor Hominis*: "so, keeping in memory the image that the Second Vatican Council has established in a perspicacious

---

1. This conciliar document strongly influences the encyclical; it is cited eleven times in LE.

and authoritative way, we shall try once more to adapt this picture to the 'signs of the times,' and also to the needs of the situation which continually changes and develops in certain directions." A little later he affirms that the Church should rediscover "the situation of man in the contemporary world, according to the most important signs of our times" (15).

In this contemporary situation not everything is positive and hopeful. The pope writes in *Laborem Exercens:* "Looking at the whole human family, dispersed throughout the earth, one can only be impressed by a *disconcerting fact* of great proportions: that, while on the one hand conspicuous natural resources are going to waste, on the other there are whole groups of unemployed or underemployed people and an infinity of hungry multitudes." But it is not enough to describe a situation; one must also go to the roots to understand the reasons for it. The pope continues: "a fact which shows beyond doubt that within political communities and in the relations among them at the continental and global levels — with respect to the organization of labor and employment — something is not working, especially at the most critical points and those of greatest social importance" (18.6).[2]

The "disconcerting fact" of unemployment and hunger (characteristics of the countries of the Third World), as well as the structural causes of those things, are a sign of the times that must be discerned in the light of faith.

To be attentive to the signs of the times means being sensitive to historical events. The human situation "continually changes"; we must recognize and evaluate those changes. The signs of the times are a summons to our reflection on the faith, because they represent a call to commitment. Before "the Church, adjusting to each generation, can respond to the perennial questions of humanity" (*Gaudium et Spes* [GS] 4), we must scrutinize the signs of the times and interpret them in the light of the Gospel.

A theology that begins with the signs of the times is a dynamic reflection, placed at the service of the ecclesial task. It is a theology

---

2. In these quotations we have kept the italics from the text of the encyclical. Our own emphases are in boldface type. In the texts of LE the first number refers to the subheading of the encyclical, the second to the paragraph within that subheading.

attentive to the historical moment in which we live. This is the type of theological reflection that *Laborem Exercens* presents to us.

On the Threshold of a New Age

Laborem Exercens is marked by an awareness that we are living in a new historical age.

Leo XIII spoke precisely of "new things" (*Rerum Novarum*) in the encyclical whose ninetieth anniversary was the occasion for the publication of *Laborem Exercens*. John Paul II underlines the continuity of the Church's teaching on social matters, but at the same time he is convinced that we are living in a different historical moment. Therefore he stresses the need to speak an appropriate word for this new situation.

He writes: "We are celebrating the ninetieth anniversary of the encyclical *Rerum Novarum* on the eve of **new** advances in technological, economic, and political conditions, which, according to many experts, will influence the world of work and production no less than the industrial revolution did in the last century" (1.3). John Paul II is clearly convinced that we are facing new realities. He continues: "The general situation of man in the contemporary world...requires us to discover the *new meanings of human work* and also to formulate *the new tasks* given in this area to every man, to every family, to every nation, to the whole human race, and finally, to the Church itself" (2.1).[3]

One new aspect of the present situation deserves emphasis, because it shows the universal perspective of *Laborem Exercens*. John Paul II recalls that "the question of social justice," concentrated in "the worker question," was seen "in the context of each nation," but recent texts of the magisterium have broadened "the horizon to global dimensions" (2.3). The pope places himself in that evolution: "if in the past, as the center of that question, the primary emphasis was on *the problem of 'class,'* more recently the focus has

---

3. And elsewhere: "work is one of those perennial and fundamental aspects, which are always present and constantly require a renewed attention and decisive witness. Because there are always **new** *questions and problems,* **new** hopes are always arising, but there are also fears and threats related to this fundamental dimension of human existence" (1.2; see also 5.6).

been on *the problem of the 'world.'* Therefore, one considers not only the class aspect but the global dimension of the tasks which lead to the realization of justice in the contemporary world" (2.4).[4]

Today not only the perspective of social class but also the question of justice has crossed national borders and requires us to consider the global dimension of injustice.[5] This includes relations between rich and poor countries, as well as the actions of multinational enterprises in the international economy. All this makes the social situation very complex. There is a constant perception of the international dimension of the issue in the magisterium. John Paul II, in his encyclical *Dives in Misericordia,* said: "it is not difficult to see that a *sense of justice* has awakened on a large scale in the contemporary world; without doubt, it emphasizes that which is in contrast to justice not only in relations among men, social groups, or classes, but also among peoples and states, among political systems, and even more among the diverse worlds" (12). The contrast with injustice appears at different levels: persons, social classes, peoples, political systems, worlds.

In these diverse areas there is a social conflictiveness that makes the situation dramatic. The pope wrote in *Redemptor Hominis:* "We face a grave drama that cannot leave us indifferent: it is always man who **on the one hand** tries to gain the greatest advantage, and who **on the other hand** suffers the damage and injuries. The drama is further intensified by proximity to the privileged social groups and to the rich countries which excessively accumulate goods, the richness of which is abusively turned into the cause of diverse evils" (16). The drama is precisely that social and economic confrontation takes place among human beings, who in principle are called to a different purpose.

---

4. That text continues: "A complete analysis of the situation of the contemporary world has made manifest in an even deeper and fuller way the meaning of the preceding analysis of social injustices; and this is the meaning that should be given today to efforts aimed at building justice on the earth, not thereby concealing **unjust structures**, but rather requiring us to examine and transform them in a more universal dimension."

5. This double dimension of the social problem, national and international, is present throughout the encyclical; elsewhere it speaks, for example, "of the damage and injustice which deeply invade social life within each nation and on an international scale" (1.2).

The pope's concern over this contrast between human groups is great. In the same section of *Redemptor Hominis* he points out, for example: "the picture of the consumerist civilization is well known, and consists of a certain excess in whole societies of the goods necessary for man — and these are precisely the rich and highly developed societies — while the rest, **at least broad sectors of them,** suffer hunger and many people die daily of starvation and malnutrition" (16).[6] Here again is the international perspective, but with a new note worth emphasizing. This is not only a matter of relations between countries. Within the poor societies there are people who participate fully in the consumerism present in the opulent countries; that is why he says it is "broad sectors" of the poor countries who suffer hunger and death. The pope is speaking about the poor people of the poor societies. His observation is precise.

All this shows that it is not enough to emphasize that the pope is placing himself in an international perspective; his considerations are also marked by the specific problems of the Third World. The first social encyclicals came primarily out of a European context. *Populorum Progressio* was a clear attempt to look from a different angle.[7] *Laborem Exercens* reinforces that viewpoint. It is not surprising, therefore, that *Laborem Exercens* produced less of a reaction in Europe than in the countries of the Third World, or to be more exact, among the poor in the poor countries, for a curtain of silence seems to have fallen over the encyclical in other sectors.

We are at the beginning of a new age in human history. The newness of this situation — with its possibilities and frustrations, with the wealth in a few hands and the misery of many — should evoke a **new** ethical reflection on these questions. The pope is aware of this new need at a theoretical level. The Church has already showed concern over these social issues; John Paul II affirms that he is speaking "in organic connection to the whole tradition

---

6. The text goes on to say that "the abuse of freedom, which is precisely related to consumerist behavior, ... today limits the freedom of others, that is, of those who suffer relevant deficiencies and are **pushed** into conditions of utter misery and indigence" (16).

7. This is the reason for the famous accusation of presenting "a warmed-over Marxism," which was made from the mecca of capitalism by the *Wall Street Journal*.

of such teachings and initiatives." But he adds, "I do this according to the orientation of the Gospel, to draw from *the patrimony of the Gospel* 'new things and old things' (Matt. 13:52)" (2.1). To go more deeply into the problem of work means "a continual updating" (3.1).

Then John Paul II writes clearly and boldly: "If in the present document we return again to this problem, . . . it is not to gather and repeat what is already found in the teachings of the Church, but rather to emphasize — perhaps more than has been done before — that human work is *a key*, perhaps *the essential key* to all social issues, if we try to see it truly from the viewpoint of the welfare of man" (3.2). It is not enough to "gather and repeat" what has already been said; one must respond to the demands of the new situation. The teaching of the Church has already concerned itself with human work, but the present state of things now emphasizes the key role that work plays in the social question.

Continuity and newness: "new things and old things." A reading of *Laborem Exercens* shows that true continuity means creativity and not a fixation on the past. The pope is fully aware that he is touching on points that have not been sufficiently present until this moment, or questions that have arisen only recently in human history.

Transforming History

The signs of the times that must be discerned by faith are historical facts. But these are not only a starting point for reflection; they are also a point of arrival, a way to verify all theoretical formulation. That is why the encyclical gives so much attention to the relationship between theory and historical reality.

If we want to abolish the perversion of putting material things above human life, it is not enough to keep in mind affirmations of principle. The distortions begin with practical actions. Says the pope: "Evidently the antinomy between labor and capital considered here . . . originates not only in the philosophy and economic **theories** of the eighteenth century, but much more in the economic-social **praxis** of that time, which was that of industrialization." And that praxis consisted of putting the means of increasing material wealth ahead of man, "who should be served by those means" (13.5). This is the perversion we are talking about. Just before this, he draws a conclusion from historical experience: "the *rupture of this coherent image,* in which the primacy of persons over things is closely safeguarded, *has taken place in the human mind,* sometimes **after** a long period of incubation in practical life" (13.3).

We are facing a "practical mistake" that distorts human work and "has caused the ethically justified social reaction" of the labor movement in defense of its rights.[8] But this mistake (forgetting the primacy of the human being in work) is not only a thing of the past: "it can be repeated in other times and places, if our thinking begins with the same **theoretical** and **practical** premises." The pope then describes the consequence of this rootedness in concrete historical behavior: "one sees no other possibility than a radical correction of this mistake unless adequate changes are made both in **theory** and in **practice**, changes that *follow the line of a decisive conviction of the primacy of persons over things,* of human work over capital as the means of production" (13.5).

With regard to "the exclusive right of private ownership of the means of production," which capitalism postulates "as an untouchable 'dogma' in economic life," the pope repeats that point of view. He writes: "The principle of respect for work requires this right to be subjected to constructive revision in **theory** and in **practice**" (14.4).

This becomes a central point of the encyclical: a change in principles and ideas is therefore insufficient and one-sided. One must go to the roots, to the place where the relationship between theory and practice is established. This leads to the question mentioned earlier, of **verification**. The encyclical says: "for this reason, a fair salary becomes precisely in every case the *concrete verification of the justice* of every socioeconomic system, and of its just functioning." For emphasis it adds: "this is not the only **verification**, but it is particularly important and is in a sense the key **verifica-**

---

8. Elsewhere he affirms that "we must frankly recognize that it was justified, *from the viewpoint of social morality,* to react against the system of injustice and harm, which cried out to heaven for vengeance" (8.3).

tion" (19.2). The justice of the social-economic system as a whole must have a concrete verification; it is not enough to base it on philosophical principles with a humanistic flavor, or on laws that recognize the rights of the poorest people. These things are important, but they remain on a formal level. This is not a matter of form but **function**; that is where the principles one affirms become true, are verified.[9]

Changes are needed, therefore, both in theory and in practice. That is the only way to correct at its roots the mistake of giving things primacy over people, which today marks the concrete living conditions of the workers. It is the only way to transform history.

A few lines to close this first section. The signs of the times are our call to reflection. This presupposes a serious understanding of the present historical moment. The encyclical refers several times to the need to keep in mind "historical experience" and "the help of the many methods of scientific understanding." All this leads to "a conviction of intelligence." This is an important conviction because the pope uses it to show the irrationality — and also the immorality — of what he calls materialism and economism, that is, the primacy of things over people. But the discernment of the signs of the times is done "above all in the light of the revealed word of the living God." Thus, what was a conviction of intelligence "acquires at the same time the character of a conviction of faith" (4.1).

But the signs of the times are also — as we have already noted — an appeal to our commitment, to our action in history. It is not enough to concern ourselves with theory; we must also be attentive to the facts. That is the reason for the demanding and challenging call for historical verification. Moreover, for Christians it is in the area of love — and in the concrete acts that express it — that our encounter with and faithfulness to the Lord are ultimately played out.

9. The pope emphasizes the importance of the verification of facts in his magisterium. Here is another text regarding concrete respect for human rights: "this is how the principle of the rights of man deeply affects the area of social justice and becomes a means of its **verification**, especially in the life of political organisms."

The Conductive Wire: Creation and Work

Theologically speaking, *Laborem Exercens* places human work in the context of God's work of creation. The pope makes this relationship explicit: "in the very beginning of human work one finds the mystery of creation. This point of departure constitutes the **conductive wire** of this document, and will be further developed in the last part of these reflections."

Thus what the pope calls the "Gospel of work" constitutes the theological nucleus of the encyclical.[10] It is an effort to place Jesus Christ at the center of the norms of social morality, with respect to human work, that are proposed in the document.

This shows the importance that *Laborem Exercens* attributes to biblical inspiration. Two sources can be distinguished in the classical social teaching of the Church: revelation and natural morality. The pope energetically underlines the first of these, the word of God, in this encyclical. He writes: "The social doctrine of the Church has its source in Holy Scripture, beginning with the book of Genesis, and in particular in the Gospel and the apostolic writings" (3.1). We have seen the importance of being attentive to the historical process of humanity, but this should be measured against the word of the Lord. Thus he says that the Church "thinks about and addresses man not only in the light of historical experience ...but above all in the light of the revealed word of the living God" (4.1).

Two observations before we go further into this matter. In *Laborem Exercens*, "biblical source" means both the Old and the New Testaments.[11] This was also true in the earlier encyclicals of John Paul II. It leads to fruitful associations and helps us to analyze the evolution of certain ideas throughout the Bible.

The second observation is that the pope not only makes numerous biblical references at the bottom of the page; he also chooses

---

10. The term "Gospel of work" appears six times in LE.

11. Of the ninety-one notes in the text, seventy-one are biblical references; they are about equally divided between the Old and New Testaments. Perhaps some specialists will comment on the absence of certain critical methods in the treatment of these first chapters of Genesis, which have been so thoroughly studied. We should remember, however, that this is a pastoral document.

one or two texts for more detailed commentary. He does this in *Dives in Misericordia* with Luke 4:16–20 (the messianic message), the texts on mercy in the Old Testament, and Luke 15:11–32 (the prodigal son). In *Laborem Exercens* he focuses mostly on the creation narrative in Genesis. In this way the other biblical citations are made, and illustrated, in the context of the interpretation he gives to the primary texts.

Thus a specific problem, in this case work, leads to a search for the biblical basis of a position on contemporary issues that is illuminated by faith. It is a reading of the word of God from within the situation that the believer is living.

The Gospel message is able to illustrate many different historical situations; we can never plumb the full depths of its meaning. This becomes clear when we read it in the context of the issues presented by contemporary reality. In Brazil the pope said this about the Church's never-ending reading of the Bible: "The Church has been meditating on these texts and messages from the beginning, but she is aware that she still has not understood them as deeply as she would wish (can she ever do that?). She **rereads** these texts and studies this message in different concrete situations, seeking to find in them a new application" (Homily in Salvador, Bahía, September 7, 1980).[12]

It is in this spirit that the encyclical undertakes a new reading of Genesis and the other biblical texts.

A Theology of the Human Person

The encyclical focuses less on work than on the worker, the person who works. The pope says: "I wish to dedicate this document to *human work,* and even more, to *man* in the vast context that work represents" (1.1).

The central biblical text is found in the first chapters of Genesis, and especially in Genesis 1:26–28, which is repeatedly cited.[13]

---

12. In *Pronunciamentos do Papa no Brasil: Texto integral segundo a CNBB* (São Paulo: Loyola, 1980), 192.

13. This is the first creation narrative, the one that establishes the fundamental equality of man and woman before God. The focus on women and work in the encyclical has been widely discussed and surely needs to be deepened. John Paul II has returned

John Paul II begins by affirming the human being as the image of God. Throughout the encyclical he relates this idea to work: "man is the image of God, among other things because he is charged by his Creator with subjecting and dominating the earth. In carrying out that mandate, man — every human being — reflects the very action of the Creator of the universe" (4.2).

The key element of this perspective had already been pointed out in *Redemptor Hominis*.[14] That encyclical affirms that the human person "is the first and fundamental path of the Church" and gives the christological basis for it: "a path that leads in a way to the beginning of all the paths that the Church must follow, because men — all men without exception — have been redeemed by Christ" (14). In *Laborem Exercens* the pope recalls this assertion and declares from the beginning that "we must constantly return to this path and always continue following it in the many aspects that reveal both the full richness and the weariness of human existence on earth" (1.1). The Church's task is to follow that path; that is the only way to be faithful to the Lord. The human being is central to the theology of John Paul II, because — in continuity with Vatican II and many contemporary theological currents — he considers that "the more the mission carried out by the Church is centered on man; we might say, the more anthropocentric it is, the more it must corroborate and fulfill itself theocentrically, that is, orient itself to the Father in Christ Jesus" (DM 1).[15] This is made very clear.

---

to this point himself. Referring to LE in a Sunday address, he said: "The problem of juridical equality between man and woman must be resolved with social legislation that recognizes the equality of working men and women." And later: "The Church recognizes and commends the specific, necessary, and irreplaceable contribution that women, especially today, can and in fact do make to the common good in the public sector and in the work sector.... Therefore I wish also to invite and encourage all women to extend the use of their precious talents beyond the private to the public social sector, and to do so wisely and responsibly" (Address of December 6, 1981).

14. In fact nn. 14–16 of RH are an embryonic form of what LE would later say about the primacy of the human being over things.

15. One sees here a reflection of the beautiful words of Paul VI at the close of the Council, where he rejected an ostensible forgetfulness of God in favor of insistence on the human person, saying: "our humanism becomes Christianity, our Christianity becomes theocentric, to such a degree that we can also affirm: to know God one must know man" (Address, December 7, 1965).

Following this path we come to the present problem of human work. *Laborem Exercens* recalls that the human being, image of God, is called to "subject the earth." This idea permits a key distinction in the encyclical, between work in the objective sense as a technical activity, and work in the subjective sense as the person who works (see 5–6). All this lays the basis for the principal affirmation of this document on human work: the human person is above things. Every perversion in the social and economic spheres derives from an inversion of these values.[16]

Redemptor Hominis had already discussed this point clearly. After affirming the need to discern the signs of the times, it says: "Present-day man seems to be always threatened by what he produces, that is, by the results of the work of his hands." And without hesitation the pope uses a technical expression to describe that situation: "The fruits of these multiple human activities are quickly and sometimes unforeseeably translated into an object of 'alienation'; that is, they are purely and simply snatched away from the people who produced them." What is worse, "at least partly and indirectly, those fruits are turned against man himself; they are or can be used against him." Thus what should be an expression of his dominion over the earth, the fruits of his work, become alien and hostile to the human person. The text continues: "This seems to be the principal chapter of the drama of contemporary human existence in its broadest and most universal dimension" (15).

"Alienation," the worker's loss of the fruits of his work, leads to the subjection of the human person to the things produced by that person. Alienation is the opposite of true human identity, because in that situation things prevail over persons. This is why John Paul continues in *Redemptor Hominis:* "man cannot re-

---

16. Paul VI had insisted in an address to the International Labor Organization (ILO) on this primacy of the human being over work. He said: "The modern conception, of which you are the heralds and defenders, is based on a fundamental principle that Christianity has especially emphasized: in work the human being comes first.... It should never again be work over the worker; never again work against the worker: always work for the worker, work at the service of man, every man and the whole man" (Address, June 10, 1969). These texts and this insistence represent an application of the words, "the sabbath was made for man and not man for the sabbath" (Mark 2:27).

nounce himself, nor can he renounce what is his in the visible world; he cannot make himself a slave to things, to economic systems, to production and to his own products." This perversion — usually a structural one — is the essence of materialism: "a purely materialistic civilization condemns man to such slavery, even though perhaps, without doubt, it happens against the intentions and assumptions of its pioneers" (16).

The pope had already reminded us that good will and declared principles are not enough; what matters is found at the level of events and realities. If things are allowed to prevail over persons, we are dealing with a materialistic conception that turns the fundamental human activity of work[17] into **merchandise** — just another thing. After affirming that "in the modern age, from the beginning of the industrial age, the Christian truth about work must be seen over against the diverse currents of *materialist* and *economicist* thinking," in *Laborem Exercens* the pope sharply notes that "for some accomplices of these ideas, work was understood and treated as a kind of 'merchandise' that the worker — especially the industrial worker — sells to the entrepreneur who is also the owner of capital, that is, the array of instruments and means that make production possible. This way of understanding work was especially widespread in the first half of the nineteenth century" (7, 1 and 2).

From the affirmation of the human person as the image of God, the encyclical moves to the heart of the contemporary problem of human work. We shall return to the meaning and other implications of this.

Finally, we shall underline an important issue in this commentary on the text of Genesis. That is the **punitive conception of work.** The biblical text affirms that as a consequence of sin, man "will eat bread in the sweat of his brow" (Gen. 3:19). This aspect

---

17. Work distinguishes human beings from animals, John Paul II says at the beginning of LE: "Work is one of the characteristics that distinguish man from the other creatures whose activity, related to the maintenance of life, cannot be called work; only man is capable of work, only he can carry it out, at the same time fulfilling his existence on earth. In this way work bears a particular sign of man and of humanity, the sign of a person active in the midst of the community of persons; this sign determines his internal character and in a way constitutes his very nature."

of work as a punishment has been recalled in many social documents; however, more recent ones have more positively accented
the dimension of work as collaboration with the creative work
of God.[18] John Paul II returns to the punitive conception, but he
adds a new and fruitful interpretation that accords with his analysis of the concrete conditions in which work finds itself today.
Weariness accompanies all human work, the encyclical often reminds us. That is the origin of the expression "the sweat of his
brow," but the pope notes that the human person is nourished by
bread "not only with personal effort and weariness, but also in the
midst of all the tensions, conflicts, and crises related to the reality of work, which distort the life of every society and even of all
humanity" (1.2)[19] The conflictive social conditions that surround
work today add yet another element to the weariness produced
by "dominion over the earth." This significant point accords with
other affirmations in *Laborem Exercens*.

The Christological Perspective

What the encyclical calls the "Gospel of work" stems from
the very person of Jesus. In its first pages the encyclical affirms:
"Christianity, broadening some aspects already present in the Old
Testament, has made a fundamental conceptual transformation:
based on the whole content of the Gospel message, and especially on the fact that he who, being God, became in all things like
us, spent most of his earthly life in *manual work* at the carpenter's
bench." This deep transformation in the concept of work begins
with the life of Jesus Christ. The text continues: "This alone constitutes the most eloquent Gospel of work." This is the first time

---

18. Commenting on the meaning of work in social teaching, especially in *Mater et
Magistra,* Y. Calvez writes: "Theologically...there are no more traces of a pessimistic
conception associating work with the punishment of sin. Certainly we cannot deny
that the punitive aspect is related to the consequences that freedom brings on itself,
when it is diverted from its original purpose and turned in on its own selfishness. But
the meaning of work should never have been focused solely on punishment" (*Eglise et
société economique: L'enseignement social de Jean XXIII* (Paris, 1963), 45).

19. A few lines earlier he speaks of: "the constant measure of human weariness, suffering, harm, and injustice that deeply pervade social life within each nation and on an
international scale."

that expression appears in the document, and its placement is significant: the "Gospel of work" is anchored in the experience of Jesus' work. That historical reality inspires the proclamation of the Good News of work.

This consideration permits us to insist on the basic distinction that we have already noted, between the subjective and objective meanings of work. Indeed the witness of Jesus, which is the basis of the Gospel of work, "shows that what determines the value of human work is not primarily the type of work that is done, but the fact that it is done by a person. The dignity of work is not primarily based on its objective but its subjective dimension" (6.5).

The final numbers of the document return insistently to this point. There it gives the christological basis of the point we noted in the previous paragraph about the relation between Creation and work. "This truth, according to which man participates through his work in the very work of God the Creator, has been particularly emphasized by Jesus Christ." That emphasis lies in the fact that Jesus, the carpenter (see Mark 6:2–3), worked with his own hands. Indeed, says the text, "Jesus did not only announce but fulfilled with his work the 'Gospel' entrusted to him, the word of eternal Wisdom. Therefore this was also the 'Gospel of work,' *because the man who proclaimed it was a working man,* an artisan like Joseph of Nazareth" (26.1).

Thus the encyclical repeats that Jesus' experience of work is at the source of his proclamation about it; but it also affirms that this experience is not something done accidentally or casually in order to show the value of work. It is something deeper: "the eloquence of the life of Christ is unequivocal: **he belongs to the world of work.**" The world of work has its own existence as a fabric of social relationships; the Son of God who became man belongs to that universe. This is a strong assertion that deserves emphasis.

But that is not all. Besides teaching this Gospel through his **actions** (including this belonging), Jesus Christ also proclaims through his **words**: "*in his parables* on the kingdom he constantly refers to human work" (26.2). Then the pope cites many examples: the work of the shepherd, the farmer, the doctor, the sower of seeds, the owner of the house, etc.[20]

This christocentric focus explains other perspectives of this Gospel of work. The creative work of God is seen in this light. Returning to the central text of Genesis, the encyclical says: "this description of creation...is at the same time, *in a certain sense the first 'Gospel of work.'* Indeed it shows the source of the dignity of work" (25.3). Other sources are added to this one: "this teaching of Christ about his work, based on the example of his own life during the years in Nazareth, is vividly echoed *in the teachings of the Apostle Paul.*" His proclamation also begins with a personal commitment and a concrete experience: "he was proud of working at a trade (he probably made tents), and thanks to this he could also, as an apostle, earn his own bread" (26.3).

Thus the preaching of Paul is placed in the context of the Gospel of work proclaimed by Jesus Christ: "the teachings of the Apostle of the Gentiles have, as one can see, capital importance for the morality and spirituality of human work. They are an important complement to this great but discrete Gospel of work, which we find in the life of Christ and in his parables, in what Jesus **'did and taught'** (Acts 1:1)" (26.4).

What the pope called the "conductive wire" — the relationship between God's creation and human work — finds its meaning and its fundamental point of reference in the life and message of Christ.

A New Way of Thinking, Judging, and Acting

The biblical position on work, which in a way is synthesized in the idea of a Gospel of work, lays the basis of a new way of looking at this issue and its implications. *Laborem Exercens* points out: "Precisely these basic affirmations on work have always arisen out of the richness of Christian truth, especially in the 'Gospel of

---

20. The pope often refers to this classical theme: the Gospel is announced through actions and words. Thus he writes in DM: "These phrases, according to St. Luke, are *his first messianic declaration,* and are followed by **actions** and **words** known to us through the Gospel. Through such **actions** and **words**, Christ makes the Father present to men" (3). See also DM 4.

work,' creating the basis of a new human way of thinking, judging, and acting" (7.1). This means, therefore, a break with the earlier way of looking at these realities.

This break and this newness establish the framework of the encyclical: that of "social morality shaped according to the needs of different ages" (3.1), as it says from the beginning. Indeed, the assumption that work is "the essential key to the whole social question" (3.2) gives John Paul II an ethical entry into the broader problem of work. He writes: "Thus we understand how the analysis of human work in the light of those words, which refer to the 'dominion' of man over the earth, penetrates the very center of the ethical-social problem" (7.4). The perspective adopted here is an ethical one. The pope insists on that.[21] In principle it is a classical issue; what is new is the approach chosen to address it. There are limits, but also strengths, in addressing it on grounds of social morality.

John Paul II is aware of those limits. He writes for example about recent historical changes: "it is not the Church's role to analyze scientifically the possible consequences of such changes in human relationships. But the Church considers it a duty to remember always the dignity and the rights of working men, to denounce the situations in which those rights are violated, and to contribute to the guidance of these changes so there will be authentic progress for man and society" (1.4). The pope cannot and does not propose a specific political program or socioeconomic system. As several commentators have noted, he is not pointing out a third way, for that would mean placing himself on a level with those systems. He is adopting an ethical viewpoint — specifically that of defending the life and dignity of the worker — in order to express a judgment on the different methods of economic and political organization. But he also emphasizes the political repercussions of an ethical perspective. Immediately after the text cited on the ethical-social problem, he affirms: "This conception should find *a central place in the whole sphere of social and economic pol-*

---

21. Another text: "there is no doubt that human work has an ethical value, which is completely and directly linked to the fact that the one who does it is a person, a conscious and free subject, that is, a subject capable of making decisions" (6.3).

icy, both within each country and in the broadest international and intercontinental relationships" (7.4).[22] But "repercussions" does not imply entering head-on — and in this case, improperly — into an economic, social, and political sphere. This is rather a matter of what *Redemptor Hominis* called premises: "a matter of the meaning of the diverse activities of everyday life, and also of the **premises** underlying many programs of civilization, political, economic, social, structural, and many other programs" (16). A discussion of the specific boundaries would be endless; many factors are at play in each case and in every circumstance. But the basic distinction between the moral sphere and social programs is clear. So is the perspective assumed in the encyclical.

The moral judgment begins with the principle identified earlier: the human person is above things. We have a particularly important historical case which should be seen in the light of this new human way of thinking and judging of which we spoke earlier. Says John Paul: "A systematic occasion, and in a way a stimulus to this way of thinking and judging, is the accelerated development of a singlemindedly **materialistic** civilization, which gives primary importance to the objective dimension of work, while the subjective — everything that refers indirectly or directly to the subject of work — remains secondary" (7.3). It is a systematic occasion and a stimulus because of its magnitude, and also because of the historical power of that society. That is the meaning of materialism: the inversion of the order of work.[23]

The encyclical's reasoning goes on implacably. Immediately it affirms: "precisely this inversion, with no recognition of its underlying program and interests, **is called 'capitalism'** in the sense which will be more broadly discussed later on."[24] Then, enter-

---

ing into surprising and historically ticklish terrain, the text affirms: "it is well known that capitalism has a precise historical meaning as a system, an economic and social system, over against 'socialism' or 'communism.' But analyzing the whole economic process, and above all the structure of production — which is what work is — one must recognize that the error of primitive capitalism **may be repeated wherever** man is treated in some way on the level of all the material means of production, as an instrument; and not according to the true dignity of work, that is as subject and author, and therefore as the true end of the whole productive process" (7.3).

There is materialistic economism wherever the human person is reduced to the level of material means of production. "One can and should also call this fundamental fallacy an *error of materialism,* since economism directly or indirectly includes a belief in the primacy and superiority of material things" (13.3). This inversion of the order of work deserves to be called capitalism, because this economic-social system created in history the most gigantic and systematic perversion of the values of work. Moreover, it is not a thing of the past;[25] unfortunately it remains current, which means that capitalism is characterized by its prioritization of things over persons (thence its materialism). Thus any system in which that happens — even if it is called collectivist or communist — deserves to be called **capitalist.** Thus apparently different ways of organizing the economy or society are criticized as "the error of capitalism."

In this case we see that by entering into social ethics, the encyclical is not hiding behind abstract principles.[26] This perspective leads to historic judgments pregnant with consequences and to bold language. It would be interesting at this point to relate this

---

25. The pope insists on the contemporary character of the capitalist mentality. Here is another text: "Despite the *danger* of considering work as a 'unique form of merchandise,' or as an anonymous 'power' needed for production (as in 'labor-power'), *it is always there,* especially when the economic problem is seen entirely in terms of materialistic economism" (7.2).

26. John Paul II writes in RH about the slavery of persons to things in contemporary civilization: "This is not just an abstract reply to the question, Who is man? It has to do with all the dynamism of life and civilization" (16).

critique of contemporary society to the ones made today from a different angle regarding the new forms adopted by international capitalism, and to "real socialism." Here we shall simply point out the importance and appropriateness of establishing that parallel.

But let us move on and see why, theologically speaking, the primacy of human beings over things permits these ethical and historical judgments. If human persons — especially the poor and oppressed — are the "measure" of human actions, it is because the Lord is present in them. This is finally the basis of Christian moral responsibility. Thus we come to the ethic of the kingdom, as it is presented by Matthew. One text of *Redemptor Hominis* is particularly clear on this point:

> For us Christians this responsibility is particularly evident, when we remember — and we must always remember — the scene of the final judgment, according to the words of Christ transmitted in the Gospel of St. Matthew. This eschatological scene must always be *applied* to the history of man; it should always be the "measure" of human actions as an essential scheme for the examination of individual and collective conscience: "I was hungry and you did not give me to eat....I was naked, and you did not clothe me...in prison, and you did not visit me." (16)

Also in *Redemptor Hominis* the pope insists on another idea in this respect. That is the concept of "social love." Let us look at one text: "the situation of man in the contemporary world seems far away, both from the requirements of justice and, even more, from social love" (16). The expression recurs in several passages of the same document, underlining the social dimension of Christian love which requires more than justice. This is the other side of what the pope had emphasized during his visit to Mexico: the social dimension of sin. For precisely in contrast to love, communion with the Lord and among human beings, it is sin that breaks that communion. Social love and social sin are the two sides of the human condition in the historical process. We know that those two aspects are disturbing to some people, but we also know that the Bible allows us to read them in the light of the free love of the Father.

Here we are applying eschatology to history. This synthesis should always be the measure of our conduct. A gesture toward our brother is a gesture toward the Lord. Now we are at the heart of the meaning of social ethics, which is the context of this encyclical.

A Church of the Poor

Number 8 of the encyclical, titled "Solidarity with Working Men," ends with a strong paragraph on "the Church of the poor." These are dense lines that need to be emphasized, but first we must put them in context.

Steps toward an Ecclesial Option

Here it is again necessary to return to the prophetic figure of John XXIII. At the time of the convocation of the Council, Pope John said — the text is worth recalling — in his message of September 11, 1962: "For the underdeveloped countries the Church is presented as it is and wants to be, as the Church for all, in particular as the Church of the poor."[27]

A few brief observations on this point. The reference to the poor countries is meaningful. For Pope John the poverty of the majorities (that is a fact) is an important factor in awakening the being and doing of the Church. He affirms, in the second place, that the Church is the Church for all. The love of God is universal, no one is beyond it; the Christian community is an expression of that love, and therefore it addresses every human person. Only in that context can we understand his affirmation, "in particular as the Church of the poor." Its universality does not contradict this preference (which is clearly not exclusive); it demands it in order to be truly universal. The God proclaimed by Jesus Christ is the God whose call is universal, addressing every human person, but it

_____

27. See the text in J. Moreno-Murillo, *Juan XXIII y Pablo VI explican el Concilio* (Bilbao, 1967), 97.

is at the same time a God who loves the poor and dispossessed with a preferential love. This dialectic between universality and particularity is a demand and a challenge to the community of the Lord's disciples.

Perhaps at the beginning few people perceived the historic power of this affirmation of John XXIII, which would lead to a whole renewal movement in the Church. But some proposed to make this issue the central theme of the Council. Everyone still remembers the incisive role of Cardinal Lercaro, the archbishop of Bologna. His profound and beautiful text has withstood the test of time.[28] There he said with needed clarity that the evangelization of the poor was not just one of the many themes that the Council must address; rather, he said, "if the Church is truly the theme of this Council, as has often been said, we can affirm in full conformity with the eternal truth of the Gospel and with the present age: certainly the theme of this Council is the Church, in its existence above all as the Church of the poor."

As a result of these reflections, the Belgian College of Rome established a working group.[29] They hoped that the Council would take as its central issue the theme of the Church of the poor, but they were disappointed. There was a beautiful text in *Lumen Gentium* (LG) 8 and other important allusions, but the issue did not become the theme of the Council, as John XXIII and Cardinal Lercaro had wished. Perhaps it was too soon.

It was the episcopal conference at Medellín that picked up the ball. Naturally so, since this was a Church that lived on a poor continent. Medellín prophetically affirmed an option for the poor and oppressed people of the continent, and proclaimed liberation in Jesus Christ. That conference was the beginning of a new direction for the Church's presence in Latin America. Puebla later energetically ratified this option and added some other important details. These meetings were the source of challenging texts, focusing attention on the evangelization and liberation of the poor. All this nourished experiences, commitments, reflections,

---

28. See the text in P. Gauthier, *Consolez mon peuple* (Paris, 1965), 198–202.
29. Ibid., 208–10.

in which the Church discovered itself with increasing vitality as a "Church of the poor."

Of course there has been no lack of problems and polemics on this point, with heated and excessive language on one side and, above all, incomprehension on the other. John Paul II dedicated an important paragraph of his encyclical to this issue, which was especially meaningful because of the immediate context (solidarity with the cause of the workers) in which he recalled the theme of the Church of the poor.[30]

Solidarity of and with the Workers

This is, as we have said, the last paragraph of n. 8 in the encyclical, titled "Solidarity with Working Men." There the pope returned to the legitimacy of the social reaction which emerged from the worker question or the "proletarian question." That reaction had led to, "almost erupted in," a great impulse of solidarity. This "was important and eloquent from the viewpoint of social ethics. It was a reaction *against the degradation of man as the subject of work,* and against the shocking exploitation of the working and living conditions of the worker for the sake of profit." The result of this reaction was to bring the working world together "in a community characterized by great solidarity" (8.2).

The pope insisted that the Church should recognize this reaction of the workers as ethically just. "Following the lines of the encyclical *Rerum Novarum* and many later documents of the

---

30. As we have already had occasion to mention, the pope insists that the Church is at the service of persons. "Man is the first and fundamental path of the Church" (RH 14). Similarly, "the Church that we all form is 'for men' in the sense that, following the example of Christ and collaborating with the grace that he has extended to us, we can come to 'reign,' that is, fulfill a mature humanity in each one of us" (RH 21). In this way the Church presents itself "to us as a social subject of the responsibility of divine truth" (RH 19). We already know the theocentric character of this humanism. This attention to the human person becomes even more demanding for the Church in the case of those who are abandoned and marginalized by unjust social structures. Referring to Christ who makes the Father present among men, the pope writes: "it is highly significant that these men are in the first place the poor, those lacking the means of subsistence, those deprived of freedom, the blind who do not see the beauty of creation, those whose hearts are afflicted or who suffer from social injustice, and finally, sinners" (DM 3, 1). The theocentricism of this option thus emphatically claims its biblical roots (see the reference to Matthew 25 in RH 16).

magisterium of the Church, we must frankly recognize that *from the viewpoint of social morality,* this was a justified reaction against the system of injustice and harm which cried out to heaven for vengeance,[31] and which weighed heavily on the working man in that period of rapid industrialization" (8.3). The protest was against the **system** and not against an occasional injustice. It challenged a "liberal sociopolitical system" which protected the interests of the owners of capital and marginalized the rights of the workers, by considering capital as the end of production and human work as a mere instrument (see 8.3).

The workers' solidarity in defense of their rights has had results. It has even "led in many cases to profound changes. Diverse new systems have been sought. Diverse forms of neocapitalism or collectivism have been developed." But, *Laborem Exercens* warns, there have also been — especially if we measure reality at the global level— "other forms of injustice, much more massive than those which, in the last century, led to the union of working men for a particular solidarity in the working world." John Paul II immediately gives examples of countries in which this has happened. These are "the countries that have already carried out a certain process of industrial revolution; also the countries where the primary place of work is in *cultivating the land* or other similar occupations" (8.4). The latter group of countries is among the poorest of the so-called Third World. And we already know the weight the encyclical gives to their viewpoint.

The important thing is that despite the changes that have occurred throughout history, profound injustices remain. They must lead to new forms of solidarity. These new forms must bear

---

31. Here John Paul II footnotes important biblical texts, whose prophetic dimension gives a special coloration to his affirmations on the reaction of the workers. These texts relate the ethical character of that attitude to the God of the Bible and refer to injustices with respect to the worker's wages. They are worth remembering. "You shall not withhold the wages of poor and needy workers, whether other Israelites or aliens who reside in your land in one of your towns. You shall pay them their wages daily before sunset, because they are poor and their livelihood depends on them; otherwise they might cry to the Lord against you, and you would incur guilt" (Deut. 24:14–15). "Listen! The wages of the laborers who mowed your fields, which you kept back by fraud, cry out, and the cries of the harvesters have reached the ears of the Lord of hosts" (James 5:4). The last text he mentions is Genesis 4:10 on responsibility to one's brother.

in mind "social groups which were not formerly included in such movements." What is happening is that those social groups have entered a process of proletarization; they "suffer, in the changing social systems and living conditions, an *'effective proletarization'* or, even more, they already find themselves among the 'proletariat,' which, although they don't yet call it that, deserves in fact to be called by that name" (8.5). Therefore the injustices which motivated the first solidarity movements at the beginning of the last century in Europe today affect new social sectors and are approaching universal dimensions.

One consequence of this is that the question of the dignity of the worker has become more compelling. That means that "to achieve social justice in the diverse parts of the world, in the different countries, and in relationships among them, new solidarity movements *of* working men and *with* working men are always needed" (8.6). At the beginning of this section the encyclical had pointed out the legitimacy of those solidarity efforts and the ethical value (the main concern of the encyclical) of that reaction. This is equally true of these new movements, but here he underlines two currents of solidarity: that which exists **among** workers and that which is established **with** them. The latter aspect broadens the panorama, calls for commitment by other social sectors, and lays the basis for what will be said later about the mission of the Church.

The Verification of Faithfulness to Christ

Before going into the details of this task, the pope unequivocally explains the meaning of this solidarity among and with the workers. It "must be always present wherever the social degradation of the subject of work, the exploitation of workers, and the spread of misery, and even hunger requires it." Exploitation, misery, and hunger; we are at the level of survival and of the most elemental right to life and justice. *Laborem Exercens* continues with a solid affirmation: "the Church is vigorously committed to this cause, because she considers it her **mission**, her service, the **verification** of her faithfulness to Christ, in order to be truly the Church of the poor" (8.6).

The *cause* is that of solidarity among and with the workers against the degradation of the subject of work and in favor of human living conditions. This is the cause to which the Church must be committed because she considers it her *mission*, her service. It is not something accidental or supplemental to her task in the world; it is precisely this commitment that *verifies* (we have already seen the importance of this notion in the encyclical) her faithfulness to Christ. Commitment to the solidarity movements that struggle for justice against exploitation, misery, and hunger is thus connected with faithfulness to the task assigned by the Lord, that is, the Church's very reason for being as an assembly of the disciples of Jesus. This commitment is therefore a proof of the authenticity of the Church's mission. This is bold, energetic language, which can give pause to those who think they see in every insistence on the Church's task in this area some form of horizontalism or reductionism.

In this context the expression "Church of the poor" takes on a very precise and compelling meaning, creatively developing the way in which Pope John used it. To consider this cause as her mission, verifying her faithfulness to Christ, allows the Church "to be truly the Church of the poor." It sets aside any compromise interpretation that would dull the edge of that prophetic affirmation. This process occurs in the heart of human history, wherever "the social degradation of the subject of work, exploitation of workers, and spreading misery and even hunger" appear. The Church will be "of the poor" if it commits itself to the cause of those who seek to abolish those inhuman situations.

Lest any doubt remain, and to avoid dallying over the complex meaning of the word "poor,"[32] the pope continues after the last sentence we quoted above: "And the 'poor' are found in diverse forms; they appear in diverse places and in diverse moments; they appear in many cases as *a result of the violation of the dignity of human work:* either because the possibilities of work are limited — that is by the plague of unemployment — or because of lack of respect

---

32. Complexity, not confusion or reduction to one of its meanings. The texts of Medellín and Puebla are clear and irrefutable on this point.

for work and for the rights that flow from it, especially the right to a fair wage, to the worker's personal security and that of his family" (8.6).[33] It is as clear as can be.

We note, and this is relevant for a country like ours with high rates of underemployment and unemployment, that among those poor there are not only exploited and badly paid workers, but also those who suffer "the plague of unemployment." Indeed they are a majority in many countries of the Third World. These are the poor to whom the phrase "Church of the poor" refers. There is no room for "spiritualization."[34] It is therefore a matter of solidarity with the real poor, "the result of the violation of the dignity of human work," and we know from the context of the whole *Laborem Exercens* and of this very paragraph that this violence has its structural causes in an unjust and exploitive system.

The beginning of the encyclical had already noted with respect to the global dimension of justice in today's world: "a complete analysis of the contemporary world has made manifest in an even deeper and fuller way the meaning of the preceding analysis of social injustices; and this is the meaning that should be given today to efforts aimed at building justice on the earth, not thereby **concealing unjust structures**, but rather requiring us to examine and transform them in a more universal dimension" (2.4). The structural causes of social injustice should not be

---

33. This is not the first time that John Paul II has explained the meaning of real poverty; he refers to it in speaking of a preferential option for the poor. The addresses of Mexico and Brazil are witness to it. There is no need to cite those texts; on the connection to Puebla, see G. Gutiérrez, *The Power of the Poor in History* (Maryknoll, N.Y.: Orbis Books, 1983), 111–65.

34. By "spiritualization" (because we have great respect for the biblical idea of "the spiritual") we refer to the stubborn and self-serving effort to erase, or replace with the deep evangelical idea of "spiritual poverty," the reality and biblical meaning of "material poverty" — thus forgetting that if we do not recognize what real poverty represents for the love and partiality of the Lord, we pervert the meaning of spiritual poverty. In truth, to affirm the one does not mean denying the other. On the contrary, to devalue the biblical meaning of material poverty is to make a subterfuge of spiritual poverty. Medellín said it well: "a poor Church denounces the unjust insufficiency of the goods of this world and the sin it engenders; she preaches and lives spiritual poverty as an attitude of spiritual childlikeness and openness to the Lord; she commits herself to material poverty. The poverty of the Church is, indeed, a constant in the history of salvation" (document on Poverty).

hidden; on the contrary they must be pointed out, analyzed, and transformed.[35]

Precisely this structural conflict is the theme of the third chapter of the encyclical and in a certain sense of the whole document, where the confrontation between capital and labor is considered the "great conflict" of our times. Once more underlining the continuing effects of this situation, the pope says: "We know that in this whole period, which has not yet ended, the problem of work has been posed in the context of the great *conflict,* which in the age of industrial development and together with that development has arisen *between the 'world of capital' and the 'world of labor.'*" This is an opposition between two worlds with the consistency and interweaving of interests and relationships that this implies; it is not a matter of impersonal universes, but rather a conflict "between the small but very influential group of entrepreneurs, proprietors or possessors of the means of production, and the larger multitude of people who did not have those means, but who on the contrary participated in the productive process exclusively through their work" (11.3).

The pope continues his analysis of the assertion at the level of the social sciences: "this conflict has arisen from the fact that the workers, offering their powers for work, put them at the disposal of the group of entrepreneurs, and that this group, guided by the principle of maximizing profit, tried to establish the lowest possible wage for the work performed by the workers." The workers know that reality from experience, with no need for ideological interpretations. John Paul II includes in this analysis an ethical judgment, which as we know is his viewpoint in this document: "we must add other elements of **exploitation**, together with the lack of job security and guarantees for the health and living conditions of the workers and their families." This also is exploitation; it is a moral injustice. It is not enough to prove a fact: the differing interests of entrepreneurs and workers, of owners and nonowners of the means of production; they must be judged

---

35. A little earlier the encyclical had denounced the situation of "millions of beings who live today in conditions of shameful and humiliating misery" (1.3). Later on the idea of "indirect entrepreneur" also implies the perception of a structural situation.

from the viewpoint of defending the life of the workers and their families.

Thus capital and labor are not abstract or anonymous forces: behind them, sustaining them, and giving them historical presence are *specific persons, social groups,* and what puts them on one side or the other is their relationship to the productive process and specifically to the ownership of the means of production. The pope's vision penetrates to the heart of the analysis, unveiling what is really at stake in the "great conflict" between capital and labor. Showing his understanding of the contemporary forms under which capitalist enterprises are managed, the pope affirms: "behind both concepts are real, living men; on the one side those who perform the work **without being owners** of the means of production, and on the other side those who act as entrepreneurs and **are the owners** of those means, or who represent the owners. Thus in the whole of this difficult historical process, *the problem of ownership* is present from the beginning" (14.1). The "great conflict" between capital and labor is the context that allows us realistically to grasp the issue of ownership, which is so much debated in the social teaching of the Church. What separates those two human groups, owners (entrepreneurs) and nonowners (wage earners), is their relation to the ownership of the means of production; the ownership of consumer goods is not at issue.

This is the "real conflict" (11.4) that is present in history. But precisely because the root of the problem is the dignity and the very life of human beings, especially of the workers, one cannot support just any solution to the problem. Every effort to resolve it must begin at that root; the only legitimate strategies are those that take fully into account the life and the most elemental rights of the worker. We are at the level of facts — which are the main focus of this document, as we have already seen; from there one can discern the value of economic and social systems, whatever they may be. Ideological judgments must come later.

This structural aspect was already clearly discussed in *Redemptor Hominis.* Speaking of the abuses which lead many to be "pushed into conditions of utter misery and indigence," John Paul makes a fruitful application of a Gospel text and affirms: "this universally known confrontation, and the contrast repeatedly cited by...the popes of our century...represent a gigantic development of the biblical parable of the rich man and Lazarus." Entering into the meaning of this comparison he shows the economic and social structures and mechanisms that are in play here, and sharply questions them. "Such a widespread phenomenon places in judgment the financial, monetary, productive, and commercial structures and mechanisms which, supported by diverse political pressures, control the world economy: they show themselves almost incapable of absorbing the unjust social situations inherited from the past, and of confronting the urgent challenges and ethical demands." The paragraph concludes: "these structures cause the continual spread of misery, and with it anguish, frustration, and bitterness" (RH 16).[36]

These considerations lead the pope to affirm — as he had already done in Mexico in 1979 — the right of workers to form associations for the defense of their rights; although the point is mentioned several times in *Laborem Exercens,* chapter 4 is particularly focused on it.

All this clearly identifies the poor who are being discussed here and the violence to the dignity of work that is questioned in *Laborem Exercens;* the same meaning is given to the expression "Church of the poor" in the encyclical. Number 8 is one of the richest and densest sections in *Laborem Exercens.* As we have seen, every word counts. It is a call to commitment, and to the verification, of the whole Church. This is a necessary condition for preaching the "Gospel of work."

Toward a Spirituality of Work

The material accumulated so far allows — and obliges — us to be brief in this last part of our exposition. The final chapter of the encyclical focuses on the spirituality of work, but we have al-

---

36. The lines quoted here refer to a note identifying as sources of these affirmations the homily given in Santo Domingo in January 1979 and the two famous addresses (reportedly rewritten during the visit to Mexico) to the Indians and peasants of Oaxaca and to the workers of Monterrey. This is significant.

ready used material from these pages to speak of the Gospel of work. Indeed the two issues are presented together. To avoid repetition we shall emphasize here only those aspects not mentioned earlier.

The first affirmation we find is that to speak of spirituality means referring to the human being as a whole. "Since work in its subjective aspect is always a personal action, *actus personae,* it follows that *the whole man, body and spirit, participates* in it independently of whether it is manual or intellectual work. The Word of the living God also speaks to the whole man" (24.1). Thus spirituality does not mean cultivating the "spirit" (a synonym for soul) as over against the body. Christian spirituality means "living by the Gospel," as St. Paul affirms. By the Holy Spirit, in accordance with the love between the Father and the Son, between God and humanity: that is the meaning of spirituality, which we must remember in order to avoid frequent ambiguities.

Work, as we have seen, is a fundamental human activity, whether it is manual or intellectual work. And this activity "enters into the work of salvation" (24.1). That is its theological location. All spirituality, all "living by the Spirit" begins with the experience of encounter with the Lord and with other people. In this case work is the location of that experience; as a distinctive action of the human being (see the first lines of *Laborem Exercens*), work puts us in relationship with God and contributes to the creation of a fraternal world. Because it is the location of our encounter with the Lord and with others, and because of its place in the work of salvation, work has — among others — a spiritual dimension, in the sense that we have recalled here.

A spirituality is a way of being Christian. A spirituality of work is a way of being Christian, marked by the experience of that human activity. This, as the pope tirelessly repeats in his encyclical, is participation in the creative work of God, and the workers "according to their own possibilities, in a sense, continue developing it and complete it, moving progressively toward the discovery of the resources and values enclosed in all creation" (25.2). We have already seen that John Paul II calls us to the creative work of God described in the first chapter of Genesis, "the first Gospel of work" (25.3).[37] The worker participates in this Gospel. Work is thus from the beginning an evangelizing experience.

In the context of the contemporary dichotomy between capital and labor, John Paul II reaffirms the worker's relation to the creative work of God. He writes: "This is **a coherent theological, and at the same time humanistic, image**." And he continues in a line that we consider relevant to the spirituality of work: "In [that image] man is the 'lord' of the creatures, which are placed at his disposal in the visible world." But this "lordship" is not unconditional: "if we see a dependency in the process of work, it is dependency on the Giver of all the resources of creation, and at the same time it is a dependency on other men, whose work and initiatives are responsible for perfecting and broadening our own possibilities for work" (13.2). Lordship, yes, but also dependency on God and other people. Work is the place where we experience this double reality that characterizes a spirituality of work. We note that the pope speaks of "our" work. We all participate in this experience.

Citing documents from Vatican II, the pope insists on a key idea with respect to spirituality: it does not relieve human beings of their responsibility to build up the world, nor to struggle for justice. And the pope affirms that *"only on the basis of such spirituality"* can we rightly understand the Church's "doctrine on the problem of progress and development." He concludes: "This is the doctrine, and the program, which puts down its roots in the Gospel of work" (26.7). We have already discussed this point and will not return to it here.

There is one more aspect which needs pointing out. Work, says the encyclical, is also a participation in the paschal mystery, in the death and resurrection of Christ. In death, because of the weariness and difficulties entailed in that human activity, which by themselves give it a salvific value. "In human work the Christian discovers a small part of the cross of Christ and accepts it in the

---

37. A brief observation. Genesis speaks of God's work, but also of his *rest*. God himself has presented the creative work itself in the form of *work and rest*. Therefore we participate in the creative work through work and also through rest.

same spirit of redemption with which Christ accepted his cross for us."

But work is also a participation in the resurrection: "in work, thanks to the light that penetrates within us through the resurrection of Christ, we always find a *tenuous glow* of new life, of *new goodness*, almost as a proclamation of new heavens and a new earth" (27.5).

This is the new earth "in which justice dwells" (27.6). The encyclical ends by relating work to the kingdom of God, the nucleus of the evangelical message. Christians should be aware of it and know "the place of their work not only in *earthly progress*, but also in the *development of the kingdom of God*, to which we are all called with the power of the Holy Spirit and with the words of the Gospel" (27.7).

Conclusion

A closing word. The last lines of the encyclical recall that although it was prepared on the occasion of the ninetieth anniversary of *Rerum Novarum*, "I have only been able to put it in final form since my stay in the hospital." This is a sober note on a painful and barbarous episode. In the weeks following the delivery of the encyclical letter, John Paul II referred several times to this document and to that painful event. He said for example, about that deep personal experience, that the event "has made me feel more intensively 'close' to those who in any part of the world and in any way suffer persecution in the name of Christ. And also close to those who 'suffer oppression' for the holy cause of human dignity, justice, and peace in the world. And finally, close to those who have sealed their faithfulness with death."[38]

To witness to Christ and struggle for justice is indeed today an occasion for persecution, imprisonment, torture, and death. Many are experiencing it in today's world. Many Latin American friends, brothers, and sisters have lived and are living these realities. That it happens so often should not numb us to the scandal

---

38. Catechesis of October 28, 1981.

it represents. But it is true that the communion of pain brings us "closer" to those people, as John Paul II says from personal experience. On the other hand, to share innocent suffering is also an occasion for prayer and for renewed service to the Gospel and the world. It is "a service of truth and love" and at the same time "a struggle and a combat."[39]

The encyclical is an expression of that service of love and truth. The role of personal experience in it seems important. Perhaps for that reason, this document also makes an energetic claim on behalf of human life and of the rights of workers. No one knows better than he, from his experience, the meaning contained in the encyclical. *Laborem Exercens* calls us to commitment, to a fight for justice, and to practical action. The pope said to the Council for the Laity, speaking of the encyclical: "Therefore I exhort you not only to study it carefully, but to put it into practice."[40] That's what this is all about.

And that call is not only to a particular region or country of the world. To smooth the edges of this text, some people suggest that he is coming from a particular national reality and addressing it alone. His affirmations are fully valid, they say, only in that context. This is a sorry effort to avoid acknowledging the call. The encyclical clearly describes the universality of the social problem, the depth of the injustice and the abandonment suffered by the poor today, the responsibility of the leaders of socioeconomic systems which violate the rights of workers, and the urgent need for the **whole** Church to make the cause of the dispossessed her own.

People may say that many things have not been explained, many points are not discussed or need further discussion, many specific options are still to be taken, paths to be followed, questions to be clarified. That is normal. It is the task ahead of us, especially the workers of the world, and especially those of the underdeveloped countries. (It is true that some sophisticated aspects of the work situation in the rich countries are not discussed in the encyclical.)

---

39. Ibid.
40. Speech of October 5, 1981.

Their suffering, struggles, and hopes are for us a challenge and a pathmark.

But this is clearly a vigorous and lucid reminder that the human being "is the first and fundamental path of the Church." It is a call based on the proclamation of a "God rich in mercy." It is a call to verification by building a Church of the poor, through commitment with the cause of today's workers, if we want to be faithful to the Lord, the "Redeemer of humanity."

— *Translated by Margaret Wilde*

- 2 -

New Things Today
A Rereading of *Rerum Novarum*

A hundred years ago, Pope Leo XIII confronted the evangelical message with the "new things" (*Rerum Novarum*) that had arisen from the industrial development of the nineteenth century. That was the beginning of what John Paul II likes to call "the social magisterium of the Church." Of course, this is a recent version of something that was always present from the first centuries of Christianity, in the so-called Church Fathers: the social dimension of the Gospel.

The clear language of Leo XIII on the new forms of misery, injustice, and exploitation created by industrialization produced complex reactions. There was enthusiasm from those who for decades had denounced this negative aspect of industrial development, surprise from the majority when they saw the Church rising above its harassment by liberal governments to speak frankly and directly about the problems of the age, and hostility in the circles whose privileges were being challenged or whose solutions were rejected. There was even resistance in Christian groups subscribing to the thesis that the ecclesiastical magisterium should not express opinions on social and economic matters. And there were some who saw in the encyclical, despite the clarity of its position in this respect, an inappropriate concession to emerging socialist theories.

Fulfilling his pastoral responsibility, John Paul II now proposes in *Centesimus Annus* (CA) "a rereading of the Leonine encyclical" (3). He knows that at the end of the twentieth century (and of

Published in *Páginas* 110 (August 1991): 7–22.

the millennium) his text may meet reactions similar to those received by *Rerum Novarum.* Therefore he recalls that the exercise of the Church's "duty-right" to speak of these matters met resistance from people "oriented to this world and this life, to which the faith should remain alien," and from those "concerned with an otherworldly salvation, which would not enlighten or guide their presence on earth." The pope rejects both these tendencies, which are still prevalent, to minimize the task of the Church; he repeats that "teaching and spreading the social doctrine of the Church pertains to its evangelizing mission and forms an essential part of its mission." He goes on to explain that this teaching embraces "daily work and **struggles for justice** in the witness to Christ the Savior" (CA 5; our emphasis).

John Paul II thus insists on the obligation and the competence of the Church to speak on social and economic issues, since they include grave ethical questions. If he embarks on this terrain it is because of the need to recall — against inertia and a false concept of efficiency — that the human person and human dignity should be at the center of every social order. Indeed the Church must be permanently attentive to new events in human history. That is what John XXIII and Vatican II called reading "the signs of the times." In the social sphere, John Paul II had done it in *Laborem Exercens* (LE), on the ninetieth anniversary of *Rerum Novarum,* and in *Sollicitudo Rei Socialis* (SRS 1987). Now he invites us to look at three points: at "the fundamental principles" of Leo XIII, "at the new things that surround us," and "at the future" on the eve of the third millennium of the Christian era (CA 3). We shall be guided by these three points in our reflections — which must be brief — on a text whose richness certainly challenges us to a more detailed analysis.

Face to Face with Reality

John Paul II reads *Rerum Novarum* (RN) in the light of contemporary concerns. The points he draws from it are still important in our time, even when they are presented under (sometimes only seemingly) different forms.

Facing a Society in Conflict

The pope correctly notes that Leo XIII saw the emergence of a new concept of the State and of authority and a new way of looking at ownership and labor. In this way "labor was becoming a form of merchandise . . . regulated by the law of supply and demand without considering even the minimum living conditions needed to sustain the person and family." Citing Leo XIII he recalls that "the consequence of this transformation is the division of society into two classes separated by a deep abyss." The result is "a grave injustice in the social reality"; Leo XIII had raised his voice against this, and against the solution supported "by so-called socialist conceptions" (CA 4).

Leo XIII sought to overcome the reality — not to deny the existence — of a "society divided by a conflict, made harder and more inhumane by its failure to recognize rules or norms." John Paul II calls it (as he did in *Laborem Exercens*): "the conflict between capital and labor."[1] This conflict extended even "to the level of physical subsistence for some and opulence for others" (CA 5).[2] The pope does not hesitate to point it out, but he does so with clarifying precision, recalling his rejection of class struggle as "a method of action" in *Rerum Novarum* and affirming that he is not condemning "each and every form of social conflict." They emerge in response to different circumstances; indeed, "throughout history, conflicts of interest inevitably arise between diverse social groups." Moreover, "facing these conflicts, the Christian must often take a coherent and decisive position." In these circumstances, choices must be made. The pope even speaks of the "positive role of conflict when it takes the shape of a struggle for

---

1. "In order to clarify the *conflict* between capital and labor, Leo XIII defended the fundamental rights of the workers" (CA 6, emphasis in the original).

2. In LE he said: "this conflict has arisen because the workers, offering their powers for work, put them at the disposal of the group of entrepreneurs, and these, guided by the principle of maximum profit, tried to establish the lowest possible wage for the work performed by the workers" (11). Later on he adds: "Behind each of these concepts [capital and labor] are living, specific men; on the one side those who perform the work without being owners of the means of production, and on the other those who act as entrepreneurs and are the owners of those means, or represent the owners" (14).

social justice."[3] The important thing is to protect the persons and respect for their rights. He says: "What is condemned in the class struggle is the idea of a conflict that is not limited by ethical or juridical considerations, that refuses to respect the dignity of the other person and therefore also one's own" (CA 14). In this case there is a confrontation that places the interest of one side above the common good, that excludes the possibility of a reasonable agreement or aspires to destroy the opponent. John Paul II therefore accurately and coherently associates it with the "total war" promoted by militarism and imperialism.[4]

In *Laborem Exercens* he had already noted the **existence** of the great conflict between capital and labor (and thus between the people who represent each side) and the class struggle employed as a **means** of resolving social injustice. The latter responds to an ideology, not to a reality, thus provoking artificial confrontations which make social relations more difficult. This is what Leo XIII and John Paul II both reject as a violation of the elemental rights of persons regardless of their social location. It is unacceptable for the bearers of a message of love.[5]

But the pope notes that this condemnation should not lead us to forget that for the social magisterium of the Church *"peace is built on the foundation of justice"* (CA 5; emphasis in the text). The true way to put an end to social conflicts is by eliminating their causes. To deny **the facts** — painful as they may be — does no good; the divisions persist and may intensify (as we are seeing today in Peru). To overcome them it is necessary to look at them face to face, call them by name, and find just solutions. *Rerum Novarum* pointed out directions in this regard, which *Centesimus Annus* picks up for our time.

---

3. On this point the pope cites his encyclical LE 11–15, and quotes a text from the letter of Pius XI, *Quadragesimo Anno*: "Indeed, when the class struggle abstains from acts of reciprocal violence and hatred, it is gradually transformed into an honest discussion, based on the search for justice" (115).

4. "This means, in a word, presenting anew — in the confrontation among social groups — the doctrine of 'total war' that the militarism and imperialism of that age imposed in the sphere of international relations" (CA 14).

5. See G. Gutiérrez, *The Truth Shall Make You Free* (Maryknoll, N.Y.: Orbis Books, 1990), 67–81.

The Preferential Option for the Poor

John Paul II affirms without hedging that issues like the conflict between capital and labor, the dignity of the worker, the right to private property, the ownership of land, labor unions, fair wages, and the critique of capitalism and Marxism belong — as we have said — "to the evangelizing mission of the Church" (CA 5). The Church "does not propose models" (CA 43); these are the task of the social and political actors and depend on specific historical situations. Nevertheless, the Church can offer a message "which becomes a source of unity and peace in the face of conflicts that inevitably arise in the socioeconomic sector" (CA 5). The Church does not have models, but it does have ethical and human demands to present (on this point see SRS 41). Not all projects for organizing society are equally valid in the light of these demands. In his view the steps taken by *Rerum Novarum* still conserve "their validity, especially with respect to the new forms of poverty found in the world" (CA 10). This poverty is the result of the exploitation and marginalization of the great majority of people. *Centesimus Annus* affirms the validity of *Rerum Novarum* on the subject of poverty at several other points, for example: "today, as in the time of *Rerum Novarum,* one can speak of inhuman exploitation" (CA 33).

There is a significant observation at the end of chapter 1. John Paul II points out that Leo XIII, more than just criticizing a particular concept of the State or a particular political theory, insisted on the need to support the most defenseless members of society. That, rather than an ideological discussion, is the heart of the matter. It is also a central and permanent issue in the history of the Church. He writes: "The rereading of that encyclical, in the light of contemporary realities, allows us to appreciate the constant concern and dedication of the Church to those persons who are especially favored by Jesus, our Lord." Here is an excellent witness to "what is now called a preferential option for the poor." As we know, this "now" comes from the experience and reflection of the Latin American Church.[6] This is the ultimate meaning of the

---

6. The expression "preferential option for the poor" emerged in the period between Medellín and Puebla and was forcefully employed at Puebla. The synod, called

encyclical whose hundredth anniversary is celebrated in *Centesimus Annus*. Therefore John Paul II understands it as an encyclical about the poor: "The encyclical on the 'worker question' is thus an encyclical on the poor, and on the terrible condition to which the new and often violent process of industrialization had reduced great multitudes of people." Unfortunately many aspects of this type of violence remain today, so he adds: "also today, in much of the world, similar processes of economic, social, and political transformation are causing the same evils" (CA 11).

It is not enough to proclaim this solidarity. The pope says: "Today more than ever the Church is aware that its social message will be made credible by the testimony of works, more than by the coherence and internal logic of its message." It is not enough to claim ownership of a social teaching; nothing can take the place of effective, daily solidarity in the struggle for justice. John Paul II goes still further; from the Church's awareness of this authenticity he derives its "preferential option for the poor, which is never exclusive, nor does it discriminate against other groups" (CA 57). As he said in *Laborem Exercens,* in making a preferential option for the poor the Church verifies its "faithfulness to Christ, in order to become truly the Church of the poor" (8). That is also how it verifies its social teaching.

Seen in this light, the social magisterium of the Church is an essential part of the "new evangelization," which the pope has been promulgating for our time ever since his trip to Poland in 1979 (CA 5).[7] The context of that magisterium is "social morality"; it is about ethical demands and not a third way between capitalism and socialism. The pope affirmed this energetically in *Sollicitudo Rei Socialis:* "The social doctrine of the Church is not, therefore, a 'third

---

to celebrate the twentieth anniversary of the close of Vatican II, says clearly: "**Since** Vatican II, the Church has become more aware of its mission in the service of the poor, the oppressed and the marginalized. The true spirit of the Gospel shines in this preferential option, which should not be understood as exclusive. Jesus Christ called the poor blessed (see Matt. 5:3; Luke 6:20), and he himself chose to be poor for us (see 2 Cor. 8:9)" (6, our emphasis).

7. It began with an address given at Nowa Huta (June 19, 1979) during the first visit to his native land. See the article by Cecilia Tovar, which carefully traces that expression in the magisterium of John Paul II, in *Páginas* 102 (April 1990): 37–54.

way' between liberal capitalism and Marxist collectivism, nor even a possible alternative to two less radically opposed solutions, but belongs to a separate category" (41). It is a separate statute, which makes it a part of the primary mission of the Church.

A New International Scenario

The historical overview to which John Paul II invited us has recalled the inspiring principles of Leo XIII; it has also allowed us to reread and express them in contemporary terms. That will help us to see the "new things" that are occurring today. This is another of the great concerns of *Centesimus Annus*. Here the pope makes a very important methodological observation. In presenting his rereading of *Rerum Novarum,* he says he wants to "place in evidence" the principles of the Church's social teaching, but he also affirms that pastoral concern has moved him "to propose an analysis of *some events in recent history.*" He considers this an obligation, but he explains: "Such an examination however does not claim to make definitive judgments, since that is outside the specific domain of the magisterium" (CA 3; emphasis in the text). We must not forget this expression of respect for the evolution of the events and for the viewpoints of Church members implied in the distinction which John Paul II makes at the beginning of the encyclical.

Recent Events

In *Laborem Exercens* and in *Sollicitudo Rei Socialis,* the pope had already pointed out the international dimension which the "social question" had acquired.[8] That framework was profoundly changed by the events of 1989 and 1990. The collapse of "real socialism" has changed the global scene. The pope attributes that collapse to disregard for human dignity, to a deeper question of "an anthropological nature" (CA 13), and beyond that to a question of relationship with God. The totalitarianism prevailing in the countries of Eastern Europe, he correctly points out, violated

---

8. In SRS he shows the importance of the North-South relationship, which also shapes the East-West confrontation (see 20–22).

fundamental human rights and smothered all personal creativity. What happened in those nations was thus caused by the people's legitimate demand for justice and freedom (see CA 23). The pope also points out that this demand was made peacefully, using only "the weapons of truth and justice." It grew out of true "struggles," but there was a determination "to try all the channels of negotiation, dialogue, and witness to the truth" (CA 23). The pope emphasizes truth, because he believes that violence seeks to justify itself with falsehood (see ibid.). His discussion on the subject of truth deserves a separate study.

These events lead to important consequences for the poor nations. The pope clearly points out the ambiguity of these consequences. The repercussions can be favorable if we take the effort to make them so; if not, the situation may not change or may even be worse for what we still call the Third World. In some ways the East–West tension was a prolongation of World War II. That confrontation entailed costs which thwarted the necessary collaboration with the poor countries; rather, these countries were manipulated in the interests of the great powers (see CA 18). The current situation opens new possibilities; what was spent on weapons can now be used to help the poor sectors of humanity. The pope believes that the resources thus released will tend to be directed to the nations of Eastern Europe. This he sees as "a debt of justice" toward those peoples; nevertheless, he observes that it would be serious if that led to "slowing efforts to lend support to the countries of the Third World."

He is right on the mark. The old tension with the socialist nations has led the United States and Western Europe to protect themselves by helping the new governments to become established and successful. But as the pope says, this would mean turning away from peoples who "often suffer much more serious conditions of insufficiency and poverty" (CA 28). The perspective of the Third World is fundamental in this encyclical.

In the 1980s we saw more than the collapse of the totalitarian governments of Eastern Europe. Little by little, "certain dictatorial and oppressive regimes" in Latin America, Africa and Asia were also falling. An important part in this process was played by the

Church's commitment *"in favor of the defense and promotion of the rights of man."* Against different types of ideology, this commitment has recalled with "simplicity and energy that every man — whatever his personal convictions — carries within him the image of God, and therefore deserves respect" (CA 22, emphasis in the text). The pope even speaks of those who have given their lives for this commitment; thus he firmly supports the witness of churches like those in Brazil, Chile, El Salvador, and all the others on this continent, and in our country, that have staked their lives on the defense of human rights.[9]

An important consequence of these changes has been, in some countries, **"the encounter between the Church and the labor movement**, which began as an ethical and specifically Christian reaction against an enormous situation of injustice."[10] Thus he introduces new perspectives for the proclamation of the Gospel. The Church, says the pope, looks favorably on a movement "oriented to the liberation of the human person and to the consolidation of their rights." In recent times "the sincere desire to take the side of the oppressed" has led many believers "to seek in diverse ways an impossible compromise between Marxism and Christianity." It is impossible because they are two very different and even opposite philosophies, with regard to their ultimate vision of history and of the human person. The pope continues: "The present time, while it has gone beyond all that was obsolete in these efforts, leads us to reaffirm the positive aspect of an authentic theology of integral liberation" (CA 26). This liberation should include the different levels or dimensions of the human being: social, personal, and religious. That theology of liberation is still needed because, as the pope explains very well, the crisis of Marxism has not eliminated injustice and age-old oppression in the world (see ibid.) The reality of the poor countries has not changed; rather it has become worse, for these peoples "now

---

9. He says, e.g., "Meanwhile in unity with the whole Church I give thanks to God for the witness, sometimes the heroic witness, which more than a few pastors, whole Christian communities, believers, and men of good will have given in such difficult circumstances; we ask him to sustain the efforts of all to build a better future" (CA 22).

10. In LE he had insisted on the ethical character of the reaction which led to the creation of the labor movement in the nineteenth century (see n. 8).

face more than ever the dramatic situation of underdevelopment, which becomes more serious every day" (CA 56).

These observations are incisive and realistic; they call us to a reflection that takes into account the diversity of social situations, the difference between intention and realization, the errors and nuances already present in these years. All this — making a careful balance of that time — will help us to make the Gospel and the Church more effectively and respectfully present in our age, especially among the poor.

The End of Ideologies?

The pope warns, in texts that will surely provoke debate, that clarity is needed about the meaning of the changes that occurred in 1989 and 1990. We should rejoice over the reaffirmation of freedom, justice, and truth that those changes represent, and over the steps now being taken by those nations toward democratic political forms and greater respect for the dignity of the human person. But this is very different from thinking that "the defeat of socialism leaves capitalism as the only model of economic organization." The pope believes that would be "an unacceptable affirmation" (CA 35). This misinterpretation would also bring serious consequences; indeed the Western countries "run the risk of seeing in that fall the unilateral victory of their own economic system, and thus failing to introduce the necessary changes in it" (CA 56).

This is not a new judgment on the pope's part. It was expressed, to the surprise of many listeners, in an address to business people during his visit to Mexico.[11] The positive elements of these events do not lead him to disavow a critical attitude; he does not fail to see the global nature and the depth of the situation. Now the encyclical deals with it in detail. A whole section is devoted to it (42).

---

11. On that occasion he said: "The recent historical events of which I spoke have been interpreted, sometimes superficially, as the triumph or failure of one system over the other, specifically, the triumph of the liberal capitalist system. Specific interests seek to carry this analysis to the extreme point of presenting the system they consider triumphant as the only way for our world, based on the experience of the reverses suffered by real socialism, and evading the necessary critical judgment on the effects produced by liberal capitalism, at least until now, in the so-called Third World countries" (Address of May 9, 1990).

The pope asks: "Can we say that after the failure of communism the triumphant system is capitalism, and that this should be
the direction taken by the countries which are trying to rebuild
their economy and their society?" Is this the model for the poor
countries that "seek the way of true economic and civil progress"?
The answer to these questions is "obviously complex." *Centesimus Annus* makes an important distinction here. If "capitalism"
means a fundamental role for business, for the market, for private property, taking responsibility for the means of production,
for freedom and creativity in the economy, the answer is positive.
The pope prefers to call this system an "entrepreneurial economy,
a market economy, or simply a free economy."

But if capitalism is understood as freedom in the economic
sphere, not subjected to a "juridical framework which places it
at the service of integral human freedom" whose center is ethical and religious, the reply is "absolutely negative." It is interesting
to see that the critique is made from the standpoint of freedom,
of which capitalist liberalism sees itself as the most genuine representative in history. The viewpoint of the encyclical is that of
a freedom which is not only total but also for everyone; personal
freedom necessarily entails a social dimension.

With respect to "marginalization and exploitation" in the Third
World, and to other forms of human alienation, especially in the
more advanced countries, the pope warns: "The failure of the
communist system in so many countries certainly eliminates one
obstacle to an adequate and realistic way of solving these problems,
but it is not sufficient to resolve them." *Centesimus Annus* insists
on this point but also warns, against any false triumphalism, of a
grave danger for our time: "the risk of spreading a radical capitalist
ideology." That risk is very much with us; indeed in recent months
we have read and heard a lot in this country about this issue.

One example at the international level is the "end of history"
thesis affirmed by an advisor to the U.S. Department of State. The
end of history would mean the irreversible and omnipotent reign
of capitalist liberalism. The pope affirms that this ideology refuses
to see the problems mentioned a few lines earlier, "because a pri-
ori it sees any attempt to face them as condemned to failure and

blindly entrusts their solution to the free development of market forces" (CA 42), that is, in a purely ideological and mechanistic way. This is like placing blind faith in the laws of history. As Carlos Fuentes has said, "Every time someone proclaims the end of ideologies, I wonder: what is their ideology?"

Immediately John Paul critically judges the situation of the poor countries and the present international order: "The obligation to earn their bread by the sweat of their brow presupposes, at the same time, a right. A society in which that right is systematically denied, and whose economic policies do not allow the workers to reach satisfactory levels of employment, cannot achieve ethical legitimation or a just social peace" (CA 43). This is what he is questioning. His phrasing is simple, but those who are determined to complicate things—in our country, for example—need to be reminded of that. Those who have ears to hear, let them hear.

Toward the New Century

This overview of the key points in the encyclical of Leo XIII has brought out an interest in rereading it; consideration of the "new things" of our time can also lead to a deeper understanding of what is happening today. This will help us to face the future; that is the orientation of *Centesimus Annus,* which "like *Rerum Novarum,* is situated almost at the threshold of the new century, and with God's help, seeks to prepare for its arrival" (62).

The Universal Purpose of Earthly Goods

In the fourth chapter, John Paul II invokes a theological theme with social significance and a long history. Significantly, the chapter is called "Private Property and the Universal Purpose of Goods." Diverse conditions in the international economic panorama have made that relationship a Gordian knot and turned that traditional theme into something fruitful and urgent for our present time.[12] God has given to all humanity what is needed for

---

12. In commenting on this paragraph, we refer to texts and considerations presented in a talk during the Jornadas de Teología at the Catholic University (February 1991), entitled "Sharing the Goods of the Earth."

sustenance. The goods of the earth do not belong exclusively to some people or social groups; they have a universal purpose. Only in that context can we accept the private appropriation of what is needed for existence and for a better social order.[13] This perspective is rooted in the Bible (see Gen. 1:28–29; Lev. 25:23–24; Heb. 2:44 and 4:32), and it is the nucleus of the position of the Fathers of the Church on this matter. Leo XIII invoked it, and it is now taken up again by John Paul II, who like the lord in the Gospel "draws from his treasure new things and old things" (Matt. 13:22) among which the Church lives (see CA 3).

The "old" is to recall, in the words of the Fathers of the Church, that the use of "goods, entrusted to one's own freedom, is subordinated to the original and common destiny of created goods."[14] This principle is not to be stated and then immediately forgotten in practice. The consequences are concrete and immediate. Human work leads to private ownership, but this is not "an absolute right, since its nature as a human right contains an inherent limitation" (CA 30).[15] The social nature of private property is a traditional theme in the Church's teaching on these matters. John Paul II has forcefully recalled it in repeated references, beginning with his inaugural address to the third Latin American bishops conference in Puebla, to the "social mortgage"

---

13. "God has destined the earth and everything in it for the use of all men and peoples. Therefore, created goods should reach everyone in an equitable way, under the protection of justice and in the company of love. Whatever forms of ownership are adapted by legitimate public institutions according to their diverse and variable circumstances, we must never forget this universal destiny of goods" (GS 69).

14. "The earth is common to all men, and therefore the food it provides are produced by all in common. Thus they are wrong to believe themselves innocent who demand for their private use the gift that God gave to all . . . when we give what is indispensable to the needy, we do not do them a favor from our personal generosity, but we return to them what is theirs. More than an act of charity, what we are doing is fulfilling an obligation of justice" (Gregory the Great, *Regla Pastoral*, 3, 21).

15. A little later he says: "The ownership of the means of production, both industrial and agricultural, is just and legitimate when it is employed for a useful purpose; but it is illegitimate when it is not valued or is used to impede the work of others or to obtain profits which are not the fruit of the global expansion of labor and social wealth, but rather of its compression, of illicit exploitation, of speculation, and the rupture of solidarity with the working world. This type of ownership has no justification and constitutes an abuse before God and men" (43).

that encumbers all private property (see also *Laborem Exercens* and *Sollicitudo Rei Socialis*).

The "new" is his affirmation that this doctrine must also be applied to another form of ownership in our time. That is "the ownership of knowledge, of technical expertise, and of wisdom." It should be noted that on these things, "much more than on natural resources, is based the wealth of the industrialized nations" (CA 32). This leads to new and profound inequalities, in which the marginalization of the poor is presented in a more disguised form. Indeed it is clear that today the great majority of people "have no possibility of acquiring the basic knowledge that would help them to express their creativity and develop their abilities" (CA 33).

This has been the dramatic experience of the poor in the countries of the Third World. It has been said, therefore, that the dependency in which they live is aggravated by neglect on the part of the rich nations. This is true not only at the international level. The problem also appears within each country. Among us, for example, the continuing deterioration of living conditions in the past twenty years, the terrible decline in the level of public education, the economic abandonment to which teachers have been subjected by successive governments, are creating two classes of people: the few, who have access to professional training through expensive private institutions (or who can go abroad), and the immense majority, who struggle to move ahead in the national (or second-rate private) schools and universities, accumulating years of study rather than knowledge. This problem has been lucidly pointed out, for example, by the council of directors of the Peruvian universities—unfortunately with little effect so far.

Also new is the return to a traditional topic which for a long time has not been understood in all its significance. The Fathers of the Church presented it as a Christian duty "to give of one's excess," but they did not understand that word as we do today. For them it did not mean "what is left over," but everything that is not *strictly* necessary for subsistence. This demand was related to the establishment of a just world. St. Augustine said, along these lines, "You give bread to the hungry; but it would be better if no one were hungry and you had no need to give it. You clothe the naked, but we should wish that everyone had clothes and there were no such need."[16] This is a question of justice and equality, not of crumbs that fall from opulent tables.

John Paul II departs from this equivocal and minimizing use of the word "excess." For him, love for the neighbor, especially for the poor, must become real "in the promotion of justice." The poor person is not a bothersome nuisance, but someone who claims a right; therefore "it is not just a matter of giving from excess, but of helping whole peoples — the ones who are excluded or marginalized — to enter the circle of economic and human development" (CA 58; see also 36). This means taking seriously the universal purpose of the goods of the earth. It is very important that the encyclical has returned, following the lines of Vatican II, to this key point from "the first social teaching of the Church." Surely this issue will be deepened and developed in the future.

Development Is the New Name for Peace

John Paul II quotes this phrase from Paul VI in his encyclical *Populorum Progressio* (CA 52), which in turn was inspired by a text from Manuel Larraín, one of the great Latin American bishops of recent decades.[17] It must be emphasized because the pope (whose concern for peace was made clear in his valiant — and lonely — position on the Gulf War) sees in contemporary poverty, and in its structural causes, one of the greatest factors of instability, both in the international order and within each country.

In many parts of the world, he points out, "the rules of primitive

---

16. This is a profoundly evangelical affirmation. The context is revealing: "In no way should we wish for evil in order to do acts of mercy. You give bread to those who hunger; but it would be better if no one were hungry and you had no need to give it. You clothe the naked, but we should wish that everyone had clothes and there were no such need. All these services, indeed, respond to needs. If we suppress the needy, that would be an act of mercy. Shall we then extinguish the fire of love? Love for a happy man, for whom you can do no favors, is more authentic: this love is much more pure and sincere. For if you do a favor for an unfortunate, perhaps you seek to raise yourself in his eyes and you want to put him below you, even though it was he who gave you the occasion to do good. Rather wish that he be your equal: together you will be subjected to him for whom no one can do any favors" (St. Augustine).

17. M. Larraín, *¿Exito o fracaso en América Latina?* (Santiago: Ed. Universidad Católica, 1965); see G. Gutiérrez, "Significado y alcance de Medellín" in *Irrupción y caminar de la Iglesia de los Pobres* (Lima: Instituto Bartolomé de Las Casas-CEP, 1989), 40–42.

capitalism still prevail, together with a shameful situation which can be compared with the darkest moments of the first phase of industrialization." In this context "one can speak today, as in the times of *Rerum Novarum,* of an inhuman exploitation." These are not isolated cases; John Paul II notes that "the great majority of inhabitants of the Third World still live under these conditions" (CA 33).

Similar situations are occurring in the rich countries. Therefore, "it is a duty of justice and truth to reverse the inability of people to meet fundamental human needs, and to prevent the death of oppressed people for the sake of those needs" (CA 34). This "opens a vast and fruitful field of action and struggle, in the name of justice, for the trade unions and other labor organizations." Things will not change without this effort. The alternative model will not be a socialist system which presents itself as "State capitalism,"[18] but a society based "on freedom of work, on enterprise and participation." Such a society would not oppose the market, but would demand that it be "appropriately controlled by social forces and by the State" (CA 35). (Neo)liberalism, which has so many supporters among us, is not the solution. Rather we must avoid falling into what *Centesimus Annus* rightly calls "the risk of an idolatry of the market" (CA 40). It is a false god, and it is not lacking for worshipers in our midst.

This idolatry leads to the alienation of human existence, that is, people's inability to own themselves. The collectivist prescription against that alienation was not only ineffective, but counterproductive. We must remember, however, that human alienation is "a reality even in Western societies": in consumption, in work, "in the diverse forms of exploitation," that is, wherever things have priority over persons (CA 41).

An example of this inversion of values is the issue of the external debt of the poor countries. With all due clarity the pope affirms that "it is not licit to demand or insist on payment, when

---

18. A socialism which gives priority to things over persons deserves to be called capitalistic, he says in LE: "this inversion of order, regardless of the program and the name by which it is called, deserves the name of capitalism" (7). On this point see the analysis of Javier Iguíñiz, "Conflicto entre trabajo y capital en la presente fase histórica," in *Sobre el trabajo humano* (Lima: CEP, 1982), 107–28.

this would impose de facto political choices which lead whole populations into hunger and despair." We see it today in our country. For this reason it is urgent "to find ways of reducing, postponing, or canceling the debt" (CA 35). On the occasion of the five hundredth anniversary there are proposals to forgive the debt of the nations of Latin America and Africa for the reasons mentioned by *Centesimus Annus* and in addition because it is seen as having been fully repaid through centuries of colonialism and economic dependence. The cancellation that John Paul II proposes lends powerful support to this claim.

An indispensable condition for healthy development is respect for nature. *Centesimus Annus* vigorously echoes a concern that is currently, and rightly, troubling many people: the ecology. Unrestrained consumerism is endangering the natural balance. Recent denunciations on the destruction of our Amazon rain forest are a case in point. Moreover, the pope emphasizes an aspect that is often overlooked: the human environment. This leads him, thinking about the problems of the large cities and about population growth, to speak of "the social ecology of work" and of "human ecology" (CA 39). This is a key point (and a new one in the social magisterium of the Church) with regard to life as a gift of God.

The Rights of the Poor

The poor not only have unmet needs; they also have possibilities and abilities to change their situation. In this case we are speaking of both poor individuals and poor nations. This requires the creation of appropriate conditions for the exercise of these abilities. Thus John Paul II calls us to "a global partnership for development," which would imply certain sacrifices on the part of "the most developed nations." This partnership must lead in the rich countries to changes "in lifestyles" which would allow all the peoples of the earth to possess a sufficient measure of human resources (see CA 52). The encyclical mentions these needed changes in lifestyle at several points, as a just demand of the human community (see also CA 36 and 58).

We are not talking about a concession. This is a demand of the marginalized people of the world: "the poor demand the right to participate and enjoy material goods, and to fulfill their ability to work, thus creating a more just and prosperous world for all." This observation is important, for it is a universal right: "the promotion of the poor is a great occasion for the moral, cultural, and even economic growth of all humanity" (CA 28). The pope believes, therefore, in the continuing need for "a great associational movement of workers, the purpose of which is the liberation and integral promotion of the person" (CA 43).

This presupposes overcoming "the individualistic mentality, so widespread in our day"; that in turn "requires a concrete commitment in solidarity and love" (CA 49). Some people, confusing modernity with individualism, see the historical perspective that begins with the poor and their right to participation, justice, and freedom as a rejection of modern values. It is not that. What it means is that when modernity encloses itself in an individualistic mentality, it becomes inhuman and ceases to be a positive factor in the establishment of a just and human world for all.

John Paul II is aware of the resistance that his encyclical will meet. But he believes that "with growing awareness that too many men live not in the well-being of the Western world, but in the misery of the developing countries and under a condition that remains an 'almost servile yoke,' the Church has felt and continues to feel the obligation to denounce that reality with all clarity and frankness, even though it knows that its cry will not always be heard with favor by everyone" (CA 61). We might add that in our countries the resistance to that "cry" will often be dissembled; it will not have the clarity and frankness of the pope's message.

As we said at the beginning, the encyclical requires a more detailed study. But by recalling some of its central points and themes we have tried to shed light on the terrible reality we are living in this country and to give hope to a people who struggle ceaselessly for their right to life, as John Paul II urges them to do.

— *Translated by Margaret Wilde*

PART TWO

The Journey
of a Church

The paths opened by Medellín have been traveled with firmness, though not without tensions, by a Church that continues to acquire a greater consciousness of the challenges facing the annunciation of the Gospel. These challenges have been manifested as much in the great episcopal assemblies (Puebla, Santo Domingo) as in the multitude of pastoral initiatives and theological reflections, the new analyses of the situation, the testimonies from life, and paths of spirituality. The perception of the complexity and the possibilities of the world of the poor is one of the most important results of this itinerary. The diversity of Latin America is a great treasure. The voices of women (especially those of the poor sectors), the indigenous peoples, mestizos, blacks, become ever more vigorous and demanding. That which comes from the marginalization that they suffer, from their hopes and joys, challenges and nourishes the faith perspective.

The density of the difficulties to be traversed, the obstacles to be overcome, the uncertainties to be dispelled do not diminish the enormous richness of this period or weaken the perspectives which are opening. The Gospel is proclaimed in the journey with others. This journey should allow us to travel without fear where the women and men of our continent live day to day with their riches and poverty. In that task, the experiences of Christians of different confessions, to their mutual enrichment, also concur.

– 3 –

The Meaning and Scope
of Medellín

An event took place twenty years ago, in the Colombian city of
Medellín, which would leave an indelible mark on the life of the
Latin American Church and society. Representatives of the different dioceses of Latin America were meeting for the second time;[1]
on this occasion there were also numerous lay people, religious,
and priests. They all brought with them the concerns, the sufferings, and the hopes of their respective peoples and communities.

In truth the Medellín Episcopal Conference did not begin on
August 26 or end on September 6, 1968; it was a result, and a point
of departure, of the journey of a people and a Church. Thus if
we reduce this assembly to its strict chronological boundaries we
will miss its significance and its scope. The assembly must be situated in this vast process, not to dilute its contribution or diminish
the content of its texts, but rather to accentuate its lines and flesh
out its insights. Two decades later, in a time that cannot be understood without it, we have a better perspective on its meaning and
its repercussions. The purpose of these pages is to trace the process
rather than to discuss the details of the assembly. We shall adopt a
global viewpoint and try to present what has risen to the top in the
intervening years as the essential contribution of that assembly.

Published in *Irrupción y caminar de la Iglesia de los Pobres: Presencia de Medellín* (Lima: CEP-
IBC, 1989), 23–72.

1. The first conference was held in Rio de Janeiro in 1955, when the Latin American Episcopal Council (CELAM) was established. There was one earlier conference:
the Plenary Council of Latin America met in Rome in 1899, with fifty-five bishops present. Their final texts were published in *Actas y decretos del Concilio Plenario de
la América Latina* (Rome: Tipografia Vaticana, 1906).

We cannot pretend to be disinterested observers of that passing scene. We are part of the process; the path taken by the Latin
American Church is our path. We are situated in its life, in the
achievements and obstacles that belong to every historical process.
This study thus begins with a profound loyalty to a Church in
which we share with others our faith and our hope. It is also important to note that our approach is marked by gratitude for the
witness of so many Christians in giving their own lives for the
proclamation of the kingdom of God. It is precisely those experiences that help us to see the essence of the message, the letter
and the spirit of the Medellín texts.

In the opening address at Medellín, Cardinal Juan Landázuri,
one of the three presidents of the conference, posed a key question: "Who are we?" He replied: "We are a part of the People
of God, in union with Christ, our only Shepherd; through the
Gospel and the Eucharist we are brought together by the Lord in
the Holy Spirit, representing the Church in Latin America,...a
Church which is trying its best to be present in the world, to listen to it, to answer."[2] This is indeed a Church coming of age,
ceasing to be a "reflection" and becoming a "source," to use the
felicitous expression of Henrique de Lima Vaz, a branch of the
People of God that is learning to be present, to listen, and to respond maturely to the challenges presented by the Latin American
reality.

Under questioning by the world in which it lives, the Church
must question its own identity. Who are we? Vatican II had raised
the question for the whole Church. How can we be in the world
without being of it? How can we be a visible sign of a deeper reality, the kingdom? Or to use the words of John XXIII: how can
we be a Church that says, "thy kingdom come"?[3]

In responding to these questions, K. Rahner has proposed a

2. "Inaugural Address" in *La Iglesia en la actual transformación de América Latina a la luz del Concilio,* vol. 1: *Ponencias* (Bogotá: CELAM, 1969), 44, 45. For translations of the Medellín documents on Justice, Peace, and Poverty, see Alfred T. Hennelly, ed., *Liberation Theology: A Documentary History* (Maryknoll, N.Y.: Orbis Books, 1990), 89–119.

3. "Anuncio del Concilio" in A. and G. Alberigo, *Giovanni XXIII profezia nella fedeltà* (Brescia: Queriniana, 1978) 276.

theological interpretation of the Council in the framework of a global understanding of the history of the Church. His thesis is that Vatican II is the beginning "of the discovery and the realization of the Church at the universal level." This event took place in the context of what the great German theologian calls the third period of the history of the Church; in it, for the first time, "the living space of the Church is the whole world" and not only the European universe.[4] Although we might debate its details and specific arguments, the force of this vision cannot be denied. It is an imaginative and stimulating perspective for understanding the present moment of the Church.

That viewpoint can help us to see what was happening in Medellín. The event affirmed, we believe, the unique personality of the Latin American Church, bringing it into full and true communion with the universal Church. Dependency, in the Church as elsewhere, creates an erosive externality and passivity. Perhaps this is helpful to those who are mainly concerned with the responsibilities and prerogatives of their positions, but it is harmful to the evangelizing presence of the wider Church on our continent. Maturity certainly has its problems and risks, but what is at stake here is our faithfulness to "Christ, the only Shepherd" and to the Spirit who calls us together as "ecclesia."

At Medellín the Church that lives in Latin America was beginning to come of age. It therefore proposed to follow a course that defines it: the preferential option for the poor. These words did not yet appear at Medellín, but the idea did. Since the conference it has been understood that way; the pastoral and theological texts containing the expression, written after Medellín, were enthusiastically recognized at Puebla. But this decision has reached beyond the continent. Medellín presented the universal Church with a demanding proposal: *the identity of the Church today leads us*

---

4. *Concern for the Church* (New York: Crossroad, 1981), 77 and 78. Theologically speaking, says Rahner, there are three great periods in the history of the Church: the time from Jesus to Paul, linked to the Jewish world; the time from Paul to Vatican II, linked to the Western universe; the third period, which begins with the Council and has a universal perspective.

into solidarity with the poor and insignificant people; in them we find the Lord who shows us the way to the Father.

This is the true meaning of what John XXIII called "the Church of all and especially of the poor." Three aspects, which are ultimately linked together and shed light on one another, are the subject of the following pages. First we shall recall the conciliar event, without which we cannot understand the contribution of Medellín. Second, we shall explore the path which the Church has laid out among us, which has been in large part a search for understanding of the people in whose midst it lives. And third, we go to the heart of the identity of the Latin American Church — and of its challenge to the whole People of God — in its evangelizing presence, in its proclamation of the kingdom to every human person.

The Horizon of the Council

With passing time, we see more clearly the importance of John XXIII in the conciliar event. Much remains to be told about why he summoned the Council and about the tasks he hoped Vatican II would take on. We need to look upstream to Pope John in order to understand our subject, the meaning of Medellín.[5]

From the beginning of his communication about the Council, we find John XXIII raising one of his firmest convictions: it is necessary to be attentive to the signs of the times if we wish, as a Church, to proclaim the Gospel of Jesus Christ. He also saw the urgency of finding adequate ways of expressing that message so that humanity can understand it in our time.

John XXIII explained the details of that concern in later texts. He recognized the need to deal methodically with the issue and therefore said that if the Council is to take the necessary "step forward" in doctrinal matters, these must be "studied and expounded in conformity with methods of research and literary formula-

---

5. Two recent works are available on John XXIII and his relationship to the Council. They are edited by G. Alberigo and include interesting studies by several authors: *Papa Giovanni* (Rome: Laterza, 1987), and *Giovanni XXIII transizione del Papato e della Chiesa* (Rome: Borla, 1988).

tion derived from modern thinking."[6] The text goes on to recall the classical distinction between the "accumulated substance of faith" and "the way of presenting" the truths contained in it. This methodological advice has been fruitful for the Council and for many documents of the magisterium in subsequent years. It responds to the pope's great concern: how should we say today, "your kingdom come"?

This same need led him energetically to reject those who were fixated on the past rather than learning from history. He called them "prophets of doom who are always announcing unfortunate events, as if the end of time were imminent."[7] It is hardly a mystery that the pope was speaking directly to people of the Church itself, as their supreme Pastor. He was trying, on the very first day of the Council, to establish the true context of that event. His warning has taken on new relevance in our time.

In the framework of his fundamental insight, the need to be attentive to the signs of the times, John XXIII proposed three great themes in different addresses prior to its opening. These are an opening to the modern world, the unity of Christians, and the Church of the poor. These points derive from the three worlds in which, according to Pope John, the Church should live and be a sign of the kingdom: the modern world, the Christian world (and more generally the religious world), and the world of poverty. The Council was more sensitive to the first two than to the third, which is understandable in the context of that time.[8]

The Modern World

To open the windows of the Church and let out "the imperial dust" accumulated over centuries is one of Pope John's most expressive descriptions of the attitude that the Council should

---

6. Address on the opening of the first conciliar session (October 11, 1962) in A. and G. Alberigo, *Giovanni XXIII profezia nella fedeltà,* 365.

7. Ibid., 362–63.

8. It is important to keep in mind the historical context of the challenges posed by these worlds and the efforts made by Vatican II to respond to them. See on this point G. Gutiérrez, "Vaticano II y la Iglesia Latinoamericana" in *Páginas* 70 (August 1985). See also G. Gutiérrez, "Por el camino de la pobreza" in *Páginas* 53 (December 1983). Some ideas for this discussion are taken from those articles.

take. Behind this call is a sharp awareness of the values of the modern world and of the negative consequences if the Church rejects them.

Of the points proposed by John XXIII, the one that received the broadest and deepest attention in Vatican II was the need for dialogue with the world. This question led to a great upheaval near the end of the first session of the Council, and it set out the path which would be productively followed in the works of this assembly. There were decisive interventions on this point from Cardinals Montini and Suenens. It not only led to the constitution *Gaudium et Spes* but established the background for all the documents.

Paul VI told the second session of the Council that in "building a bridge to the contemporary world," it should be aware of the limits and shortcomings as well as the values of that world; the Church has much to learn from them. The overall goal is service to that world. With solemn and penetrating words the pope affirmed: "let the world know: the Church sees it with deep understanding, with true appreciation, sincerely desiring not to conquer it but to serve it; not to disparage it but to value it; not to condemn it, but to comfort and save it."[9] These are profoundly evangelical terms which express both humility and confidence in the Church's task — attitudes which are sadly missing in our day.

That was the context of the Council, with a truly impressive variety and richness of theological approaches and pastoral criteria. This is not the place to list them in detail; we will mention only one thorny and important issue, because of its immediate impact on the point we are discussing. The world to which the Council was opening was above all the world of modern science and technical expertise; it was also the world of democracy, human rights, and the modern freedoms demanded in the previous two hundred years, especially in Europe (although this does not diminish their universal scope). In a word, it was the Western and primarily North Atlantic modern world.[10]

---

9. Address on September 29, 1963, in John XXIII and Paul VI, *Discours au Concile* (Paris: Centurion, 1966), 107.

10. The ambiguities of the modern world are pointed out in some texts of the Council, but in general this critique is not developed. Little is said, for example, about the

This opening therefore meant incorporating important secular and democratic values, in their broadest and most fundamental sense, into the reforms proposed by the Council for the Church itself. This was a different context from the exercise of responsibilities assigned by ecclesial structures.

To the world, the Church boldly presents herself as the "universal sacrament of salvation" (LG 49). It is an efficient sign in human history of God's salvific will toward all human beings and the whole human being. We don't need to insist here on the newness of this ecclesiological perspective; there was resistance to it in the conciliar assembly, but it would leave a lasting imprint on the life of the Church. This perspective has since become the fruitful context for reflection by the Church present in Latin America, on its role in the process of liberation.

The Christian World

An opening to Christians of other confessions was another great concern of John XXIII. Like the opening to the world, it first met a cool reception from the people responsible for preparation, but was later enthusiastically embraced by the Council itself. Ecumenical dialogue was surely one of the richest, most prominent features of Vatican II and the early postconciliar period.

Moreover, following the recognition of salvific values in other Christian confessions, there was an opening toward Judaism and a new understanding of the great human religions.[11] This too required building bridges and adopting an attitude of service toward people of other spiritual families. It has affected our understanding of the Church and its role in history; but beyond that it implies a humble and respectful relationship to the saving action of the Lord, even beyond the visible boundaries of the Church.

The Council responded to these challenges, in line with the concept of the Church as a universal sacrament of salvation, by

---

negative impact of the values of Western society on the causes of the poverty and marginalization in which the majority of humanity lives. The situation at the time called for a generally optimistic tone.

11. See, for example, the misgivings and critical observations raised on this point by Cardinal J. Ratzinger, *The Ratzinger Report* (San Francisco: Ignatius Press, 1988).

returning to the old question of the relationship between institution and community. Communion is a fundamental theme of the conciliar ecclesiology, which gives full meaning to the legitimate and traditional affirmation of the visibility and institutionality of the Church. Indeed, Vatican II seeks to establish a fruitful link between those two aspects of the Church as a sign of the kingdom.

The ecumenical question has had less impact on the Latin American Church than did the question of an opening to the world. Given the relatively small presence of other Christian confessions (with some exceptions, and especially in comparison with Europe, North America, and other continents), this perspective was a direct concern only in minority sectors. However the underlying attitude of opening and dialogue, which strengthened the previous point on the contemporary world, was warmly received. Indeed, ecumenical dialogue is full of rich consequences for the concept of the Church and its mission, which was especially relevant to the search that was taking place at the time in Latin America.

We should note that for several decades the Church had been preparing the way for both the opening to the world and the ecumenical opening. Many pastoral experiences, and substantial theological reasoning, had taken place with regard to both issues. These were the responses of certain ecclesial circles, especially in Europe and North America, to the challenges posed over centuries by the separated brethren and the contemporary society. These experiences, contacts, and ideas contributed greatly to a warm reception of Pope John's first two insights. Many of the people who had spent their lives working in this direction were present at the Council; for some of them these efforts had caused painful difficulties within the Church, but they finally played a key role in Vatican II. Their earlier reflections, placed at the service of the Council, formed the backbone of what John XXIII called its *punctum salens:* not "the discussion of this or that article of the fundamental doctrine of the Church," but "movement toward a doctrinal penetration and a formation of consciences" around the new problems.[12]

---

12. Opening address in A. and G. Alberigo, *Giovanni XXIII profezia nella fedeltà*, 365.

The World of the Poor

The third topic suggested by John XXIII, the Church of the poor, was not as well developed in advance as the first two. For that reason, and because the problems of the Third World were only beginning to be raised in the Council, Pope John's third insight left only a faint mark on the conciliar documents. It was however a wholehearted response to the challenges that the Latin American Church faced, and continues to face.

The Law of the Kingdom

John XXIII raised the question of the Church of the poor one month before the beginning of the conciliar sessions. He began by recalling that Christ is our light and that the Church should understand its service to humanity in that light. To this effect he noted some important points: the equality of all peoples in the exercise of their rights and obligations, the defense of the family, and the need to move beyond individualism and assume a social responsibility. To this the pope made a surprising addition: "Another enlightening point. The Church presents herself to the underdeveloped countries as she is, and wants to be: as the Church of all and particularly the Church of the poor." A few lines later he spoke of "the miseries of social life that cry out for vengeance in the presence of God."[13]

John XXIII liked the image of an "enlightening point" as a way of emphasizing an idea (see the proclamation of the Council [January 25, 1959] and *The Diary of a Soul*). The September message is a brief text, but one in which every word counts; its sober modesty should not lead us to overlook its fundamental character. These words, and the lifetime witness of a free man like John XXIII, were the beginning of a profound and greatly encouraging ecclesial movement: a process which continues today with advances and reverses, for all its possibilities have not yet unfolded.

As we have already recalled, the first conciliar session marked a turn in the path followed by the Church. In the abundant and creative effervescence of ideas that grew out of the insights of

---

13. Message of September 11, 1962, in ibid.

John XXIII, many new directions were taken which transformed the framework established by the preparatory commissions. One important direction came from the archbishop of Bologna, Cardinal Lercaro: in one noteworthy intervention, which deserves more detailed analysis, he elaborated on the theme of the Church of the poor.[14] Here we shall mention only a few of his points.

With a lucidity and foresightedness that still amaze us, Cardinal Lercaro affirmed: "this is the hour of the poor, of the millions of poor who are all over the world; this is the hour of the mystery of the Church, mother of the poor; it is the hour of the mystery of Christ, especially in the poor." Therefore, "the most profound need of our time, including our great hope of promoting the unity of all Christians, will not be satisfied but rather evaded if the evangelization of the poor in our time is treated at the Council as one theme among others." Indeed "this is not just a theme, but in a sense the only theme of Vatican II." Earlier he had pointed out that the evangelization of the poor is "the synthetic element, the point of clarification and coherence of all the points that we have discussed and of all the work that we must carry out." To go deeply into the issue of the Church of the poor would be the most faithful response to the first two great themes raised by John XXIII: dialogue with the modern world and Christian unity.

The profoundly theological perspective of this intervention is worth noting. It shows not only Cardinal Lercaro's sensitivity to the social aspects of poverty, but also his concern with placing Christ at the heart of the whole issue. He said: "The mystery of Christ in the Church is always, and particularly today, the mystery of Christ in the poor; because the Church, as his holiness John XXIII has said, is the Church of all, but today especially it is the Church of the poor." This aspect of the mystery of Christ present in the poor "is the constitutional law of the kingdom of God," and therefore full of consequences for the daily life of the Church and of those who bear responsibility in it.

---

14. See the complete text, with valuable notes, in G. Lercaro, *Per la forza dello Spirito: Discorsi conciliari,* a cura dell' Instituto per le Scienze Religiose (Bologna: Edizioni Dehoniane, 1984), 109–22.

The urgency of this theme for the archbishop of Bologna is expressed in his frequent references to it. He said in a report to Paul VI: "The call to evangelical poverty today has become more than an essential element of the perfection and beauty of the Church and of the witness to universal Christian brotherhood; evangelical poverty is rather an absolute condition, purely and simply expressed, for the **historical survival** of the religious sense of the world and of life."[15] Thus the archbishop of Bologna explains the thinking of John XXIII (to whom he had close personal ties) and removes any ambiguity that the expression "Church of the poor" might have if it is taken out of context.

On the Path of Poverty

Working groups formed around these ideas were very active in the corridors of the Council, but were not very successful in bringing this perspective into the documents. *Lumen Gentium* 8, sought to gather these concerns in a rich christological text, but a brief one: "as Christ carried out the work of redemption in poverty and persecution, so also the Church is called to follow the same path in order to communicate the fruits of salvation to men."

We also have the beautiful text of *Ad Gentes* (AG) 5: "Just as this mission continues and develops throughout the history of Christ's own mission, who was sent to evangelize the poor, the Church, impelled by the Holy Spirit, must follow the same path as Christ, that is, the path of poverty, obedience, service, and self-sacrifice unto death, from which he emerged victorious through his resurrection."

These texts are carefully focused on poverty in the life of Christ. They both refer to the evangelization of the poor, and *Lumen Gentium* bases that mandate on the fact that the image of the Lord is visible in them. Puebla later picks up that evangelical theme and expresses it with energy and beauty (31–39). In both cases poverty is discussed as "a path" which was taken by Christ and should again be taken by the Church in its historic journey.

---

15. "Apunti sulla povertà" (November 19, 1964), in ibid., 162 (our emphasis).

Thus it is not a goal or an ideal, but a means by which to give an authentic evangelical witness.

Despite the value of these texts and a few others, we are clearly a long way from Cardinal Lercaro's proposal to make the "Church of the poor" (an expression not found in Vatican II) the theme of the Council. Clearly the time was not yet ripe for this issue, in contrast to the others raised by John XXIII: the need for the Church in the modern world and in the Christian (and more generally the religious) world. As we have said, the most active participants in Vatican II felt more comfortable and better equipped to deal with these two points. Nonetheless, the perspectives of the Council have created space for experience and reflections along the line of the Church of the poor.

In Search of Latin America

The years between Vatican II and Medellín (from 1965 to 1968) were an intense period in the life of the Latin American Church. From a distance we see this period as a search for Latin America by a Church that until then had been oriented away from this continent.

One fundamental condition of maturity is to know the terrain in which we live. That was the challenge to the Church on this continent in the aftermath of the Council, and it became one of the most important tasks in the preparation for Medellín. It happened along two converging lines. The richer and more important of these was shaped at meetings of the departments of CELAM, created under the leadership of Manuel Larraín; inspired by an authentic conciliar spirit, each department brought together representatives of the diverse estates of the People of God (bishops, lay people, religious, priests) around a theme of burning importance for the ecclesial task. These events produced important texts and created a vibrant fraternal atmosphere for the Medellín conference. The other line was necessarily more subdued, but it also had sharp repercussions. That was the immediate preparation carried out by CELAM and the commissions assigned to the task at that time; an important aspect of this was the elaboration of a "basic preliminary document" which was sent to the different national dioceses.[16]

The Road to Medellín

During the time of the Council only select groups in Latin America were concerned with the daily events at the Vatican assembly. Most Christians perceived only slowly the changes that were occurring in the Church, except for the liturgical changes. It was very different in Europe, for reasons that are easy to explain. Vatican II touched on questions that were being actively raised among Christians in the rich countries; naturally these questions also affected our continent, but to a lesser degree.

Manuel Larraín, the bishop of Talca, Chile, who is surely one of the most prominent figures in the Latin American hierarchy of our time, clearly perceived this situation. Near the end of the Council Don Manuel, who was president of CELAM at the time (Dom Helder Camara was the vice president), conceived the idea of a Latin American episcopal meeting to study our situation in the light of Vatican II. That meeting was held years later at Medellín. His insight was correct. Although not everyone realized it, Latin America was beginning a process of deep change.

Responding to Poverty

In November 1965, shortly before the end of the Council, Don Manuel organized a meeting between CELAM and Pope Paul VI. His intention was to make this interview a first step in the preparation of a Latin American episcopal conference.[17] The address the pope gave on that occasion was particularly inspiring for the process he sought to begin.[18]

---

16. Published in *Signos de Renovación* (Lima, 1969), 193–215.

17. I remember that Don Manuel said in Rome during the last phase of the Council: "What we have lived here is impressive, but if we in Latin America are not attentive to our own signs of the times, the Council will bypass our Church, and who knows what will happen then."

18. Paul VI asked Don Manuel, whom he held in special regard, for a memorandum of ideas to use in preparing his address to CELAM. Months later, shortly before his death, the bishop of Talca called this message a "pastoral encyclical" for Latin America. He called that text "a prophetic cry which can awaken even passive spirits to the new winds of the times. It is, in a word, the Church's response to the anguish and

Following the clear line of the Council, he advised the bishops always to keep their "eyes wide open to the world...because the world is changing, and we need to know how to meet its growing needs and interpret its new demands." A Church closed in on itself is unable to fulfill its evangelizing task. This task requires a strong community, able to face new situations, willing to make the needed changes within itself. Paul VI did not hesitate to point out what he saw as negative aspects of the Church in Latin America, saying: "One can speak of a state of organic weakness, which shows the urgent need to revitalize and reanimate Catholic life, to give it more substance in doctrinal principles and more solidity in practice. One might say that the faith of the Latin American people has not yet developed to its full maturity."

To describe the present situation as an "organic weakness" is to call for a needed self-affirmation, for maturity in the faith of the people of God in Latin America. Only in this way can we face the challenges of a world which requires us to keep our eyes open. The pope made clear what he saw as the central issue: "It is the social aspect which most seriously affects and concerns the world in general and the Latin American world in particular, where there are intense and profound differences. The anguished cry of so many who live in inhuman conditions cannot leave us unmoved; within the limits of our abilities, we can and must hear and respond to it."[19]

To respond required a Church truly present in the world in which it lived, aware of itself and possessing its own identity. The task, the destiny of the Latin American Church, was at stake on the question of poverty. The journey to Medellín had begun.

A Blood Tax

Months before this address by Paul VI, Don Manuel Larraín had called attention to the meaning and implications of under-

hopes of a continent which is seeking a definitive and absolute solution for its problems. The address of Paul VI to Latin America has the value of a sign of the times that we must understand" ("Respuesta de América Latina" [Address to CICOP, June 1965] in M. Larraín, *Escritos completos* [Santiago: Ediciones Paulinas, 1976], 1:453.

19. Address of Paul VI to the Latin American Episcopal Council, November 23, 1965.

development in Latin America and throughout the Third World. This prophetic bishop saw underdevelopment as one of the gravest threats to world peace; poor peoples are more familiar with that threat than with the nuclear one that—with good reason—worries the great powers and rich nations. Larraín was reading the international situation from the viewpoint of the poor sectors of humanity. He wrote: "This is just as immediate and permanent as the atomic bomb, and in my judgment, even more serious; for the peoples of the Third World, underdevelopment means war for today or tomorrow."

Don Manuel also explained that this war is not merely a possibility; it is an already present event. He reminded the large nations, and Latin Americans who are sensitive to what is happening in our midst, that poverty is a greater killer than World War II. The victims in this case are the people of the Third World. He said forcefully:

> As many people die every year from misery, and from the hunger and disease it causes in the Third World, as died in the four years of World War II. Every year, underdevelopment kills millions of human beings. Never in history has there been a crueler battle. This blood tax, paid by the underdeveloped world, is a scandal that cries out to the Father in heaven. We Chileans, we Latin Americans are not threatened by atomic weapons; we neither know nor possess such weapons. The threat to our peace, we repeat, is underdevelopment.

What is the reason for this underdevelopment? Don Manuel asked. The answer is complex. He emphasized historical factors: "Political independence, achieved at the beginning of the last century, did not bring with it economic and social independence. In the political order we became sovereign peoples, but we remained in economic and social 'colonialism.' "[20]

The problems are clearly identified. His way of presenting them

20. M. Larraín, ¿Exito o fracaso en América Latina? (Santiago: Universidad Católica, 1965), 5 and 14.

naturally shows the influence of the themes being discussed at the time, but beneath those formulations we can see his fundamental insights. The Latin American perspective was sharp and clear; he was determined to engage the Church in the challenges of that reality.

Don Manuel's ideas inspired a meeting organized by CELAM in Mar del Plata, Uruguay, in November 1966. Sadly, the bishop of Talca died in an accident a few months earlier. The meeting did not go very far in analyzing the causes of poverty in Latin America, but it gave an interesting emphasis to the role of Latin American integration. One of its conclusions was that "integration in Latin America is an ongoing and irreversible process. It is an indispensable instrument for the harmonic development of the region and marks a fundamental stage in the movement toward the unification of the Human Family."[21]

Populorum Progressio (March 1967) had a greater impact on Latin America than did Mar del Plata. In that letter Paul VI used a cherished idea of Don Manuel Larraín: "Development is the new name for peace." Several of the themes neglected in Vatican II, from the viewpoint of the poor countries, are present in this encyclical. It was said in those years that the encyclical was something like a *Gaudium et Spes* for the Third World. Besides its influence on social matters, *Populorum Progressio* was also relevant to the understanding of the faith. At a theological level, the notion of integral development presented by Paul VI stimulated the perception of liberation in Christ as a single, holistic event; this understanding was present from the beginning of the discourse on faith that has evolved since then in Latin America.[22] For these reasons *Populorum Progressio* was one of the documents most often cited at Medellín. It surely marked an important step forward in the social teaching of the Church.

---

21. *Presencia activa de la iglesia en el desarrollo y en la integración de América Latina* (Bogotá: CELAM, 1967), 17.

22. This debt is explicitly recognized in G. Gutiérrez, *Theology of Liberation* (Maryknoll, N.Y.: Orbis Books, 1988), 162; see also *The Truth Shall Make You Free: Confrontations* (Maryknoll, N.Y.: Orbis Books, 1990), 119–20.

The Poor, Agents of Their Own Destiny

The most important event in recent decades of Latin American history has been the new visibility of those who were always oppressed and neglected. Poor peoples have begun to stand up for their right to life and dignity; through their adversity and uncertainty they seek to take the reins of their destiny into their own hands.

A New Historical Consciousness

The 1950s marked the beginning of a better understanding of socioeconomic reality in Latin America. We have already discussed the theme of underdevelopment; it led to a clearer picture of the poverty in which the immense majority of the Latin American population lives. But soon the perspective we call "developmentism" revealed its great weaknesses: in particular its acceptance of the model of development offered by the rich countries and its failure to analyze the causes of poverty.

Dependency theory, formulated by Latin American social scientists in the mid–1960s, helped to overcome those weaknesses. Despite the limitations we see in it now, that theory led to qualitative progress in the study of the social order prevailing on the continent. Perhaps its main contribution was to make clear the need for structural analysis, that is, the need to go beyond a simple description of the reality. Dependency theory was a global and historical approach to underdevelopment.

This approach became a part of ecclesial thinking at a meeting of the Department of Social Action, held in May 1968 at Itapoán, Brazil. That meeting got to the heart of the matter:

> To carry out structural reforms in Latin America, leading to the development of 'the whole person and all people,' we must first see clearly the true nature of the evil to be eradicated: underdevelopment. It is a fallacy to think that underdevelopment is caused only by the lack of technical expertise and capital or by a shortage of other resources: it is a global social issue which can only be understood as a his-

torical phenomenon, directly related to Western industrial expansion.

The participants focused on the dependency in which the Latin American countries are living: "It also follows that underdevelopment can only be understood in relation to dependency on the developed world. The underdevelopment of Latin America is largely a **byproduct** of capitalist development in the Western world." They were referring to the dependence of the poor countries on the rich countries, but more specifically to the situation of the poor in the poor nations, because the privileged classes are generally in complicity with large interests at the international level.

> It is a fact that we are in a system of international relations in the capitalist world, and more specifically, at the periphery of an economic space in which the Latin American nations revolve like satellites around the **center**. The oligarchies in each country, whose interests and values are identified with those of the international imperialism of money, help to maintain this status quo which benefits them, and therefore help to perpetuate external dependency and the impoverishment of our countries.[23]

To move beyond underdevelopment, therefore, means breaking that dependency. The perspective of Itapoán became a great influence on Medellín, especially through the section on the Latin American social situation in the basic preliminary document for that conference (January 1968), although in general the merely descriptive focus of the document avoids discussing the causes of poverty.

By Their Own Strength

But there was something in those years even more important than the new understandings of reality. That was a growing awareness that the liberation of the poor and oppressed can come only

---

23. The document of Itapoán is found in *Signos de Renovación,* 31–45.

from them. The Message of the Bishops of the Third World (August 1967) made that abundantly clear. The purpose of this text was to respond to *Populorum Progressio;* half the signers were Latin American bishops, especially Brazilians. On the subject at hand, the message said:

> The people of the poor and the poor of the peoples, among whom the Merciful One has placed us as Pastors to a small multitude, know from experience that they must rely on themselves and their own strength, rather than on the help of the rich.... First and foremost it is the poor peoples and the poor of the peoples who must work for their own advancement.[24]

"By their own strength." That is indeed what the people of Latin America were beginning to learn in those years: it is a hard way, but it has only been reaffirmed in more recent times. The presence of a poor people, in the process of becoming the subject of its own history, was on the horizon of Medellín. Much of the weight of the Medellín texts comes from this conviction, which was just dawning at the time. It was already present at one of the first meetings of the CELAM departments to which we referred earlier, the one held at Buga, Colombia (February 1967), to discuss the Catholic universities. The final text of that meeting reflected experience in popular education, especially in Brazil. The innovative work of Paulo Freire was an especially important influence.

The focus of liberating education was to help the poor to take control of their own destiny and their own liberation. The Buga document affirms:

> In this situation, education is becoming an integral part of the upward movement of the popular classes, and is taking their liberation, within a project of national renewal, as its principal task. The great and urgent tasks of education

---

24. The text of this document is in Hennelly, ed., *Liberation Theology: A Documentary History*, 48–57.

in this phase all point to the release of the creative energies of the whole human person: the energies of a people, most of whom are still in a situation of economic, political, and cultural dependency, subjected to arbitrary groups or interests.[25]

This meant taking education beyond the narrow limits of instruction, understood as a warehousing of knowledge ("the banking system of education," as Paulo Freire called it). Education was becoming part of the historical journey of a people struggling for life and for their rights. This certainly was not the classic approach of the Catholic universities. The newness of its ideas, and the surprise they evoked, made Buga an important landmark on the way to Medellín.

Toward a New Evangelization

The period before Medellín and later the conference itself were infused with a fundamental concern: how to proclaim the Gospel in Latin America. A new awareness of the situation of misery and exploitation, sensitivity to the desire of the poor for liberation, and the conviction that they must become the agents of their own destiny, all help us to understand the Church's unique role as a sign of the kingdom.

The preparatory document for Medellín — deficient in its analysis of social reality, but very interesting from a theological and pastoral viewpoint — points clearly to an insight that John Paul II has again taken up in recent years. The document said: "Free of the temporal bonds to which the Church is not called: free of inappropriate partnerships, which she rejects; free of the burden of ambiguous prestige, which does not serve her interests, the Church seeks to undertake **a new evangelization of the continent**."[26]

This was the central concern of Medellín, carried over from the previous stage and now formulated as "a new evangelization." John Paul II referred to this concern in the context of the

---

25. *Los cristianos en la universidad* (Bogotá: CELAM, 1967), 40.
26. In *Signos de Renovación*, 215 (our emphasis). See also the Message of Medellín.

"half millennium of evangelization," speaking about the need for "a **new evangelization**. New in its fervor, in its methods, in its expression."[27]

Medellín was the beginning of that new stage in the proclamation of the Christian message in Latin America, but it still needed to be accelerated and deepened. The basic document clearly pointed out a necessary condition for evangelization: the Church must renounce its doubtful social privileges and place itself at the service of all, beginning with the poor and oppressed. We have seen clear signs of that commitment, and of its costs, in recent years. Thus the perspectives opened at the time of the Medellín conference are still very relevant.

Human History on the Horizon of Salvation

To respond to the challenges of poverty, as Paul VI urgently told the Latin American bishops near the end of the Council, requires the Church in its pastoral practice and theological reflection to read that cruel reality in the light of faith. In other words we must place that reality on the horizon of salvation in Christ. In this way a theme that was opened up in the theology of that time, and which was present at the Council, was brought back into the Latin American context and contributed to the necessary reading.

We refer to the perspective that emphasizes the fundamental — but not monolithic — unity of history, in the sense that every person is called to communion with God and with others. This unity does not permit confusion between the aspects we call temporal and religious. Indeed the difference between those dimensions should not lead us to think in terms of two histories; that would imply a devaluation, from the viewpoint of faith, of the tasks involved in establishing a just and human world. The affirmation of unity also should not lead us to forget that salvation in Christ is a free gift, and that human freedom enables us to say yes or no to that gift. This unitary approach is especially prominent in two important texts from the pre-Medellín period.

---

27. Address to CELAM in Haiti, March 9, 1983.

The preparatory document recalls that "man's fulfillment be-comes complete in the salvation that Christ brings. For by lib-eration from personal and communal selfishness, through con-version, salvation leads humanity to personal, conscious, and free communion with God, with their brothers, and with the world. The death and resurrection of Jesus Christ liberate humanity from sin and death, and from all the consequences and characteristics of both: ignorance, disease, misery, and the different forms of op-pression." This text later inspired a famous passage in the Medellín document on Justice (3).

The text clearly affirms the provisional character of all historical events: "this full salvation that God carries out through Christ is being fulfilled in human history, but it will not be total and defini-tive until history ends in the fulfillment of the kingdom of God (see LG 40)." But it also insists on the presence of the kingdom today: "nevertheless this very kingdom is already present among us, giving meaning to the things God is doing among people, leading them by the outpouring of the Holy Spirit into the res-urrection of Jesus, and thus into participation in the life of the Trinity."

The *already* but *not yet* full presence of the kingdom underlies the basic unity of history. In it human beings

> give a free response to this salvation offered in Christ. Some accept it, others do not. They accept it in some way, even if they do not explicitly know Jesus Christ, when moved by a secret Grace, they attempt to go beyond their selfishness and open themselves to the task of building this world and enter-ing into communion with their brothers (see GS 22; LG 16). They do not accept it when they refuse to recognize this obligation of human promotion, service, and communion. This is a sin. Because of human limitations, human deci-sions and historical actions often bear the double seal of an effort to respond to even an unknown God, and of selfish withdrawal from their brothers.[28]

---

28. *Signos de Renovación*, 212.

The deepest chasm in human history is the one between grace and sin. In grace human beings accept God's call: to reject it is sin, because it means refusing to make love the ultimate meaning of one's life. This idea was again taken up in one of the richest, most fraternal and creative meetings held prior to Medellín. In April 1968, the CELAM Department of Missions called a meeting in Melgar, Colombia, to reflect on the missionary task of the Latin American Church. The department was led in those days by Gerardo Valencia — bishop of Buenaventura, the Colombian port city where he exercised his pastoral ministry — whose devoutness and prophetic stature have left a deep mark in the memory of the poor people who made up his diocese and of everyone who knew him. The theoretical framework of Melgar was shaped by one of the most theologically solid documents of Vatican II, the inspiring decree on missions *Ad Gentes,* which successfully reflected the reality of the continent.

At Melgar there was also a clear affirmation of the fundamental unity of history, and at the same time a recognition of what that implies for the situation of poverty and injustice and for the search for liberation.

> All the dynamism of the cosmos and of human history; the movement for the creation of a more just and fraternal world, for the overcoming of social inequalities among people; the efforts, so urgent on our continent, to liberate people from all that depersonalizes them: misery, ignorance, hunger; and the growing awareness of human dignity (GS 22) have their origin, are transformed, and are perfected in the salvific work of Christ. In him and through him salvation is present in the heart of human history, and in the final analysis, every human act is defined by that salvation.

These ideas are closely related to the working document; at the same time, the main themes that would be present at Medellín (poverty, justice, liberation) are organically linked to the perspective of total salvation in Christ. Nothing escapes the liberating action of the Lord; that is the firmest conviction of this text. Moreover, the presentation follows a sequence that would later become familiar in the theology of liberation. The passage cited above speaks of a movement for liberation which begins by over-coming social injustice, continues with a new awareness of human dignity, and culminates in full communion through the salvific action of Christ. These three dimensions of liberation, as we have already noted, are presented as a unitary but not monolithic process. Puebla would later take up this idea in a literal form (321–29).

Also, since this is a missionary text, Melgar shows a concern for those who do not explicitly confess faith in Christ. The document explains: "There is a partial acceptance of communion with God when people, even without explicitly confessing Christ as Lord, are moved by grace (LG 16), sometimes secretly (GS 22; AG 3), to renounce their selfishness and seek to create an authentic human fellowship. There is no acceptance when people are unconcerned with building the world, do not open themselves to others, and intentionally turn inward upon themselves (Matt. 25:31–46)."

The perspective here, as in the basic document, is Christ-centered. The active presence of the grace of Christ makes human events a history of salvation, without infringing on the autonomy of those events. Melgar says with brilliant clarity:

> the saving energy of the death and resurrection of Christ, present in humanity, makes human life a history of salvation in which different religious groups play diverse parts; this also includes those of our continent, in different ways. Because whatever truth and grace are found among the peoples as a veiled presence of God, whatever good is sown in the human mind and heart and in the cultures of the peoples, not only doesn't die but becomes healed, raised up, and completed in order to be returned to its author, Christ, through the missionary activity of the Church (AG 9).[29]

The text reveals a deep sense of the freeness and the universality of the saving love of God.

---

29. Ibid., 117–18.

A Missionary Perspective

Melgar forcefully recalled the presence of those who are perpetually absent in Latin America: the Indian peoples and the black population. They are a challenge to Latin American society and also to the Church; both have tried to shape themselves without considering the existence, the culture, and the values of these peoples. One expression of this attitude is the pretense that there is no racism in Latin America; that pretense is one of our greatest social lies. Melgar makes it clear:

> In Latin America, along with the dominant Western-style culture, there is a great plurality of cultures and a cultural amalgamation of Indians, blacks, mestizos, and others. These cultural differences are not sufficiently known or recognized in their languages, customs, values, and aspirations. The integration of these groups into national life is often, unfortunately, understood more as a destruction of their cultures than as the recognition of their rights to develop, to enrich the cultural patrimony of the nation, and to be enriched by it. (Melgar 3)

This insight from the Melgar meeting was not sufficiently considered at Medellín. It remained an open question. But pastoral work in the Indian world continued in the following years, along with theological reflection on that work. Puebla would later echo those concerns; this was only a nudge on a long and controversial journey.

The destruction of which the text speaks began five centuries ago. The approach of the five hundredth anniversary later became an excellent occasion for addressing this concern. With a fearless look at history, Medellín spoke of the Church's responsibility in those complex events:

> This present awareness turns toward the past. On examining it, the Church rejoices in the work carried out with such generosity and expresses her recognition of those who have plowed the furrows of the Gospel in our lands, who have been actively and lovingly present in the many cultures, es-

pecially the Indian cultures of the continent, and to those who have continued the educational work of the Church in our cities and rural areas. The Church also recognizes that throughout her history not all members, clergy or laity, have been faithful to God's Spirit. Looking at the present, the Church rejoices in the commitment of many of her children, and also sees the fragility of her own messengers. She respects the judgment of history on those lights and shadows, and assumes the full historical responsibility that falls on her in the present. (Introduction, 2)

The missionary spirit of Melgar goes beyond the perspective of a simple pastoral adaptation to seek creativity in proclaiming the Gospel message:

To be therefore attentive to human life, to the dynamism of the people's personal and collective history, and to respect the cultural and religious values (GS 92) of the people who are reached by missionary action (LG 17) is not only a matter of pastoral adaptation; it means above all discovering the way in which Christ is already fulfilling the plan of salvation which includes everyone. Only in this perspective is the discernment of values possible. (Melgar 3)

The christological focus of the text emphasizes the universality of the work of salvation and discerns the values of cultures and religions.

An Evangelizing Presence

The year 1968 was a difficult one in Latin America. The Brazilian dictatorship was in its most aggressive period; the military regime in Argentina was harshly repressing the popular movement; Mexico was experiencing the terrible massacre of Tlaltelolco. The twilight of the Belaunde government in Peru and the Frei government in Chile held out little hope, and conflict was intensifying in Bolivia and Colombia. Oppressive and corrupt governments persisted in Haiti, Nicaragua, and Paraguay. These situations only aggravated the deep and perpetual poverty of the Latin American people. So in that year we were far from feeling the euphoria that some have attributed to Medellín.[30]

In these circumstances the preparatory document called for a new evangelization. Medellín assumed this perspective courageously and prophetically; although its message took some people by surprise, the conference — as we have noted before — was the result of a process. By force of circumstance, it was a short and intense stage in Latin America of what has been a long and complex journey in the history of the universal Church. Medellín germinated in the Church, but it was also nourished by the sufferings and hopes of the Latin American peoples. That was the source of its power and impact, and also of the resistance it encountered in the privileged social sectors.[31]

A central point at the Medellín conference was the method adopted for the drafting of documents. John XXIII had called attention to the signs of the times. Medellín responded, using the framework that had developed in the lay apostolic movements: see, judge, and act — in other words: a vision of reality based on the appropriate disciplines, the corresponding theological reflection, and, finally, pastoral guidelines in response to the first two stages. This methodological perspective greatly helped the Latin American Church to grow to maturity as a sign of the kingdom.[32]

We want to emphasize two aspects: sensitivity to the deep anx-

---

30. I think there is no facile optimism in the closing sentences of an article on Latin America that I wrote in 1969: "We now face an uncertain future, in which the only certainty is that the Spirit will lead us to the full truth: that is the perspective of hope. Or perhaps for now in Latin America, the perspective of hope 'against all hope.'" G. Gutiérrez, "De la iglesia colonial a Medellín," in Víspera 16 (April 1970): 8.

31. See the early critical articles by A. Lleras Camargo in Visión (Mexico City), September 19, 1968, and May 9, 1969.

32. It has been said, falsely and maliciously, that Medellín was excessively influenced by those who were there as expert advisors. The following authoritative witness is worth recalling: "It is naive to interpret Medellín in terms of pressure from a handful of experts, who allegedly induced such a large and representative group of bishops to sign the documents. A similar (and unfounded) rumor circulated around the Council. It is also unjust to imagine that Medellín was made by a handful of bishops; although there, as in similar events, some may have been more active than others and the leadership of some may have emerged or become manifest" (A. López Trujillo, "Una mirada global," in Medellín: Reflexiones en el CELAM [Madrid: BAC, 1977]).

iety of the poor on the continent for liberation and, by way of response, the emerging face of a Church in solidarity with them.

The Cry of the Poor for Liberation

To read present reality in the light of faith we must first have a close understanding of the situation; we must go beyond appearances and perceive what is really at stake. Medellín did that by focusing on the theme of liberation, which was the focus of many people's efforts in those years. It did not remain at the anecdotal and inevitably ambiguous level of those efforts. Rather it went to the heart of the matter and thus sought an understanding that "we are at the threshold of a new historical age on our continent, full of desire for total emancipation, for liberation from all servitude, for personal growth and collective integration," and called for the courage to enter fully "into the painful birth of a new civilization" (Introduction, 4).

The Rights of the Poor

The great concern of Medellín was the proclamation of the Christian message in words and action. Its analysis of reality, its theological reflection, and its pastoral perspectives showed that clear and urgent concern.

To proclaim the Word of God requires an understanding of people and of the social context in which they live. Medellín moved resolutely in that direction, giving "attention to the people of this continent, who are living in a decisive moment of their historical process" (Introduction, 1). To those who preferred a Church disengaged from the real, everyday situation of the children of God, the bishops explained from the beginning — referring to Paul VI and to the Council — that "in this way the Church has not 'turned away' but rather has 'returned' to the person" (ibid.).

This "return" to real people marked the life of the Latin American Church in those years, provoking the hostility of some, but also hopeful expectation among the great majority. Their reality is described as "painful poverty, in many cases close to inhuman misery" ("Poverty" 1); it is judged ethically as "a situation of injustice" ("Peace" 1), and theologically as "a situation of sin" (ibid.).

Medellín did not stop with a description of the reality of poverty. Following the line of Itapoán, it sought to point out the causes; the only way to attack evil is at its root. Thus it drew on the theory of dependency, which at the time was gaining currency in the Latin American social sciences. It fearlessly denounced unjust social inequalities, in particular "in those countries marked by a two-class structure, in which a few people have plenty...while many have very little" ("Peace" 3). Later, John Paul II would deepen this perspective in his opening address at the Puebla conference and point to a direct causal relationship in speaking of "the rich who grow richer at the cost of the poor who grow poorer." All this added up to what the bishops, both at Medellín and at Puebla, called a situation of "institutionalized violence."

To refer to social conflictiveness ("a grave structural conflict," as it was later called in Puebla 1209), does not mean relishing or promoting it; that would be inhuman and unchristian. For the Latin American bishops, it simply meant looking at things as they are, in order to contribute to their transformation by means of the Church's own task: the proclamation of the Gospel. The Church's faithfulness to the message of Christ was at stake.

Moreover, the tensions recognized here included not only those between social classes, but also between races, cultures, and with regard to the unacceptable situation of women, especially in the poor sectors. Medellín was equally concerned with international contrasts and with those occurring within the Latin American countries.

But the bishops' description of Latin American reality also went beyond its conflictive aspects. They were attentive — their analysis would be defective otherwise — to the existing values of the Latin American people and to their possibilities of radically and humanely transforming a status quo that "cries out to heaven." It was precisely one of the objectives of Medellín to base its analysis on these riches and potentialities for the establishment of a new world for all. This means that the poor and disinherited become aware of their situation and their possibilities of transforming it.

The conference documents repeatedly call for the organization of the poor in order to build a just society. Far from all paternalism, Medellín placed its trust in such organization, desired it, and defended it. This was one of its most innovative points, and most disturbing to those who refuse to see the reality or who pretend to look for change "from the top down," as if a transformation that respects the life and freedom of others — the indispensable condition for all change — could come from those who today enjoy economic, social, and cultural privileges.

Medellín is an invitation, ratified at Puebla, for people to join efforts without forgetting "the rights of the poor and oppressed" ("Peace" 22). One of these efforts is to be the artisans of their own destiny, responsible actors in a new society. Its insistence on this point is one of the most significant characteristics of Medellín.

Avoiding a False Peace

To speak of "institutionalized violence" (Puebla picks up that expression and also uses a synonym: "institutionalized injustice") does not mean opening the doors to all kinds of violence. Quite the contrary: Medellín was aware of the inhumanity of what Dom Helder Camara called "the spiral of violence." To point out the first violence does not justify others, but calls attention to a fact in order to go to the root of a situation that can go out of control, as is happening today in Peru.

This brings us to an important point. At Medellín violence (in its different expressions) was discussed in the context of a message of peace. Facing a situation of tensions and contradictions it is even more urgent to build peace, authentic peace. To live Christian love for all people is a fundamental demand of the Gospel. This was a deep conviction of the people who worked on this theme.

Confrontation with the Gospel shows the need and the demands of peace as a condition of authentic human life, as well as a condition of a society which respects, against all types of authoritarianism, personal freedom and the participation of all in leadership. To build peace is to eliminate violence wherever it comes from, by eliminating its causes. The peace message of

Medellín is gaining new relevance on a continent that is bleeding, and desperately questioning its future.

On this point the conference presents an important theological reflection in one of its best texts, the document called "Paz" ("Peace"). It points out three marks of the peace that must be built in Latin America:

a. "Peace is above all the work of justice" ("Peace" 4). If there is no social justice, there is no peace. Medellín explains that "peace in Latin America is not, therefore, the simple absence of violence and bloodshed." This is certainly important, but it will be a false peace if we try to build it on the ruins of the most elemental human rights. That is what the bishops meant when they wrote: "The oppression exercised by the groups in power can give the appearance of maintaining peace and order," a simple and deceptive appearance that refuses to build true peace on the basis of a just order.

b. "Peace, in the second place, is a permanent task" ("Peace" 14). Peace does not mean resignation or passivity; it is "a struggle, an inventive skill, a permanent goal." That is the opposite of a "static and apparent peace which can be obtained by the use of force." Christians are artisans of peace, but as we have seen, the document repeatedly warns against an illusory peace that is only a way of maintaining "personal and collective injustice." To build a just order requires going beyond inertia and dogma, beyond the imposition of ideologies; it requires freedom and imagination.

c. "Finally, peace is the fruit of love" ("Peace" 14). Love, which does not separate God from persons, is the first requirement of the Gospel. On that basis a just order must be built which is the only guarantee of peace. In that sense Medellín affirms: "love is the soul of justice." Work for justice and peace must be moved by real love for real persons. The bishops deepen this perspective, and with the inspiration of Matthew 25 they warn that wherever there are "unjust social inequalities... there is a rejection of the gift of peace; more than that, a rejection of the Lord himself" (ibid.).

We can say that the Medellín proposal for peace is a call to truth: a challenge to avoid the deception of a false peace that seeks to disguise the inhuman situation of the poor on this continent.

That kind of peace does not work in any case, because in the words of Paul VI cited at Medellín, social injustice is "the continuous and inevitable seed of rebellions and wars." Those whose storehouses, desire for power, or vanity are fed by the current situation do not want to hear talk of that reality. Nevertheless, true social peace cannot be attained without looking that reality in the face. The bishops at Medellín were grounded in a profound biblical perspective when they said that a situation of disregard for the right to the life of persons is in the last analysis a rejection of God. Peace based on justice is an aspect of the liberation to which the poor aspire in Latin America. This call to truth made at Medellín blows forcefully against the storm of social lies that is gathering in Latin America, attempting to hide the real conditions of life and death experienced by the poor.

The Gospel of Liberation

Medellín counters the situation of institutionalized violence and death with the Christian message as "word of life" ("Catechesis" 15). But for this "it is not enough to repeat or explain the Message. Rather the 'Gospel' must be expressed without ceasing, in new ways, in relation to the forms of human existence, keeping the human, ethical, and cultural environments in mind and always remaining faithful to the revealed Word" (ibid.)[33]

Here Medellín moved in a direction that John Paul II would later call the gospel of liberation. In a letter to the bishops of Brazil he wrote: "The poor of this country, who have you as their pastors, the poor of this continent are the first to feel the urgent need for this **gospel of radical and integral liberation**. To hide it would mean defrauding and disillusioning them" (April 1986, our emphasis).

The bishops took up the cry of the poor for "a liberation that never reaches them" ("Poverty" 2). Puebla later would describe this cry as "clear, growing, imperative, and sometimes threatening" (89). It is a deep aspiration of all peoples, especially of the

---

33. The document *"Catechesis"* was enriched by the important meeting organized by the CELAM Department of Catechesis a week before Medellín.

poor. But it is not enough to hear the cry; it is also necessary to respond with the Christian message and with historical effectiveness. That requires a clear awareness of the radical and global nature of the redemptive action of Christ. Poverty and injustice are not merely social questions, but represent a severe challenge to the Church: "The poverty of so many brothers cries out for justice, solidarity, witness, commitment, effort, and endurance for the full achievement of the saving mission assigned by Christ" ("Poverty" 7).

Following the lines of the working document and the Melgar meeting, Medellín sets liberation in the framework of the saving work of Jesus. "It is God himself who in the fullness of time sends his Son, made flesh, to liberate all people from all the forms of slavery to which they are subjected by sin." Immediately it specifies "ignorance, hunger, misery, oppression" ("Justice" 3). In a Christian context, sin means a lack of love for God and the neighbor, a turning inward to oneself and one's own interests. The final root of social injustice lies in that severing of friendship. For that reason, as the text makes clear, what theology calls sin cannot be separated from the situation of misery and oppression. This theme is a starting point and central focus of the theology of liberation.

Establishing that point deeply and unambiguously was one of the most perceptive contributions of Medellín. For that very reason it was also a major point of reproach by those who insist on an ahistorical view of religion. But Vatican II had already made that connection, and Puebla would later ratify it in many ways. Here too, the truth hurts.

Early on — on the way to Medellín and later at Puebla — the theology of liberation embraced a formula to express this reading of the desire for liberation in the light of the Gospel: *total or integral liberation*.[34] The goal was to set Christ's salvation, with all its transforming power, at the heart of a vast historical movement

---

34. The concept is already present in the basic document: "humanity, the object of all the concerns of the Council, is also the center of all the efforts of the Church in Latin America. For that reason the Church seeks totally to embrace human anguish and hopes, in order to offer the possibilities of a full liberation and the riches of integral salvation in Christ, the Lord" (*Signos de Renovación,* 210).

of liberation. This movement cannot be limited to a supposedly exclusive liberation in the religious sphere, forgetting the other dimensions of human life. That would be a betrayal of its purpose: to guarantee true freedom for all. Liberation, the substantive way to freedom in Latin America, is a very complex challenge. It entails risks, but also challenges and promises.

It is equally dangerous to reduce the message of Christ to its historical and political dimensions. That mutilation and deformation of the Gospel must be firmly rejected. Medellín was very clear on this point, precisely because it insisted on the social scope and dimensions of salvation in Jesus Christ: "For these reasons we seek a Latin American Church that evangelizes the poor and shows solidarity with them, witnessing to the value of the goods of the kingdom, and humbly serving all the people in our countries" ("Poverty" 8). Indeed one cannot eliminate the danger by avoiding the commitment required by the Gospel, but rather by means of a constant and critical discernment based on faithfulness and creativity.

A Church in Solidarity

In response to the cry of the poor for liberation, Medellín proposes a Church in solidarity with their aspiration to life, freedom, and grace. One beautiful and far-reaching text says that the conference seeks to present "the face of an authentically **poor, missionary, and paschal** Church, detached from all temporal power and boldly committed to the liberation of the whole person and every person" ("Youth" 15, our emphasis). "Poor," "missionary," and "paschal" denote three paths that begin with the love of God and express the Church's solidarity with every person and especially with the poorest people. The three terms also expressed solidarity with the liberation movement that was evolving among the Latin American people, to which the Church seeks to contribute through faith in the God of life.

Sacrament of Salvation in a Poor World

What must the Church do to be a universal sacrament of salvation in a world marked by poverty and injustice? This is the great question raised by the Council and Medellín for many Latin American Christians. Puebla also sought to respond to this question.

It means confronting the "inhuman misery" ("Poverty" 1) that we referred to earlier. Both the effects and the causes of this situation must be examined in order to eliminate its social and economic roots. This is a conflictive reality, in which the kingdom of life must be proclaimed. As the Council foresaw, it means following "the way of poverty" (*Ad Gentes* 5). Medellín speaks of it as a "poor Church," which precisely in order to be a sacrament of salvation must commit itself to the poor and to poverty.

The document "Pobreza de la Iglesia" ("The Poverty of the Church") explains the concept of poverty by making a distinction that has marked Latin American reflection on this subject:

- "Poverty as a lack of worldly goods is, in itself, an evil. The prophets denounce it as against the will of the Lord, and in most cases as the fruit of human injustice and sin."

- "Spiritual poverty refers to Yahweh's poor. Spiritual poverty is an attitude of openness to God, the self-offering of those who wait on the Lord for all things. Although it values worldly goods it is not attached to them, and it recognizes the higher value of the goods of the kingdom."

- "Poverty as a commitment that voluntarily and lovingly assumes the condition of people in need in this world, to testify to the evil that it represents and to spiritual freedom with regard to worldly goods; this follows the example of Christ who took upon himself all the consequences of the sinful human condition, and who 'being rich became poor' for our salvation."

Facing this situation and these demands, "a poor Church:

- "Denounces unjust deprivation of the goods of this world, and the sin that engenders it;

- "Preaches and lives spiritual poverty, as an attitude of spiritual childlikeness and openness to the Lord;

- "Commits herself to material poverty. The poverty of the Church is, indeed, a constant in the History of Salvation" ("Poverty" 4–5).

The text clearly establishes a rejection of material poverty when it means a lack of the necessities for a life of dignity and humanity. At the same time it resolves any ambiguity about the concept of spiritual poverty, which is seen as spiritual childlikeness — certainly one of the deepest themes in the Bible. This distinction helps us to understand the true meaning of the commitment to poverty.[35]

In Latin America in our time this perspective has led to many commitments and experiments by local churches, Christian communities, and religious communities, seeking to witness to liberation in Christ in the world of the poor. It is not an easy task. Indeed it means a radical change of perspective, which can be achieved only through a process. There has been progress in this search but also setbacks, encouragement but also discouragement, successes but also failures.

In the task of proclaiming the Gospel, Medellín calls for "effective preference for the poorest and neediest sectors, and to those who are segregated for any reason" ("Poverty" 9). This requires "a sharpening awareness of the obligation of solidarity with the poor, to which we are led by love. This solidarity means taking on ourselves their problems and their struggles, knowing how to speak for them" ("Poverty" 10).

The texts we have just cited are found in a paragraph with a meaningful title: "Preference and solidarity." These are two relevant points in the message of this conference. Medellín saw from the beginning that preference for the poor does not entail neglect of that other fundamental evangelical principle: the universality of Christian love. At the beginning of its pastoral guidance, it says that the Church seeks to be "humbly serving all the people in our countries" ("Poverty" 8).[36] Puebla later ad-

---

35. See Gutiérrez, *Theology of Liberation,* 162–73.
36. This affirmation is repeated several times in the same document (see n. 18) and in other Medellín texts.

dresses the issue, inspired by Medellín and by Latin American theology.

The theme of the Church of the poor at Medellín, and in the pastoral practice and theological reflection that build on its texts, has a specifically christological focus. It is not only about sensitivity to the real situation of the immense majority of poor who live on the continent; the fundamental demand, and the one which gives the deepest meaning to the whole issue, comes from faith in Christ. The Medellín document on Poverty makes this very clear. We shall cite only one of many texts on this point: "The poverty of so many brothers cries out for justice, solidarity, witness, commitment, effort, and struggle for the fulfillment of the saving mission assigned by Christ" (7). Salvation in Christ, of which the Church is a sacrament in human history, is the ultimate foundation of the Church of the poor.

This christological perspective is also inspired by an affirmation of Vatican II. *Lumen Gentium* says that the Church "recognizes in the poor and those who suffer, the image of its poor and long-suffering founder...and seeks to serve Christ in them" (8). This identification of Christ with the poor (see Matt. 25:31–46) is a central theme of reflection on the Church of the poor. Puebla expresses it beautifully in a long text, speaking of the features of Christ that are present in "the very real faces" of the poor (31–39).

That is, the Latin American Church (in its magisterium, pastoral practice, and theology) adopts a theological perspective on the theme of the Church of the poor. To speak of that Church not only means accentuating the social aspects of its mission, but refers above all to its very nature as a sign of the kingdom of God. That was the heart of the insight of John XXIII ("the Church is and seeks to be"), developed by Cardinal Lercaro. It is important to emphasize this, because there is a tendency to see these subjects as a "social problem" and to believe that the Church can deal with the meaning of poverty through a secretariat on social issues.[37]

This is not the way to understand the Church of the poor in

---

37. At the closing of Medellín Cardinal Landázuri said: "What we call 'social action' in the pastoral context of our service to the People of God as bishops is neither an appendage, nor opportunism, nor sentimentalism. We will be faithful to our ecclesial

Latin America. That concept is deeply faithful to John XXIII and to the influence of his ideas in the Council.

An Evangelizing Urgency

Medellín affirms that the Church must be not only poor, but missionary. This was a broad perspective at Vatican II; we can even say it was the great inspiration of the Council's texts. It means a Church turning outward from itself to serve the world, and ultimately to serve the Lord of history, as we read in *Gaudium et Spes*.

This missionary spirit is very well expressed in *Ad Gentes*. There the mission is presented — in a trinitarian perspective — not as a discrete activity of the Church, but as a central feature of the whole Christian community. Medellín identifies with that line as a Church that has lived, in its own way but to some degree comfortably, with Christendom. Let us examine two points that have marked the life of the Latin American Church in this regard.

a. The deep and demanding evangelical theme of proclaiming the Gospel to the poor was present at Vatican II, but as we have seen it did not become a central issue. It was central at Medellín; that was the context of the preferential option for the poor that inspired the greatest texts of the conference.

We are familiar with the biblical bases of the proclamation of the Gospel to the poor. What needs to be emphasized here is that this perspective has marked the life of the Latin American Church in our times. Many ventures and commitments have been undertaken to carry out that proclamation of the message to the disinherited. It was along this way that the Church discovered the deep aspiration for liberation of the poor on this continent.

All this has meant a great renewal in the action of the Church. The missionary requirement always implies coming out of its own world and into a different one. That is what has happened to important sectors of the Latin American Church when they set out to evangelize the poor and oppressed: they began to discover the

---

calling in the degree to which we follow, in our spirit and our pastoral dynamics, the words of Paul VI: 'the poor, sacrament of Christ' " (*Signos de Renovación,* 252).

world of the poor. It was a reality much more alien to the Church than it realized, a world with deprivations and limitations, but also with possibilities and riches. To be poor means surviving rather than living;[38] it means being subjected to exploitation and injustice, but it also means a way of feeling, of thinking, of loving, of believing, of suffering, of praying. To proclaim the Gospel to the poor means coming into their world of misery and hope.

The Church in Latin America has not gone far on this path. But the process has begun, with a kind of openness to the world, in this case, as the Council put it, to the universe of the poor. This perspective has also become a place of fruitful encounter with Christians of other confessions, which has opened new paths to ecumenical dialogue.

These efforts are incipient but real. Other churches in Latin America can say what the Peruvian bishops recently affirmed of their own experience: "This message of liberation in recent years has inspired the life of the Peruvian Church and many pastoral documents of the Episcopacy; it is a source of spiritual deepening. The Church has achieved a meaningful presence in the whole society as a sign of hope and salvation, especially in the poorest and most marginalized sectors."[39] But that presence entails new challenges, which can be met only with increased Christian maturity in the Spirit.

b. Second, new perspectives have been opened through years of commitment to the defense "of the rights of the poor according to the evangelical mandate" ("Peace" 22), and the creation of Christian base communities as "the first and fundamental nucleus of the base, which must...be responsible for the richness and the growth of the faith" (Medellín, "Joint Pastoral Planning" 10).

---

38. See John Paul II, Address to the Peruvian Bishops (October 4, 1984). The poet and musician Atahualpa Yupanqui tells this beautiful and sad story: "Once some travelers met an Indian and asked him for a chicken to eat. The Indian answered them: 'No *papay,* we don't have chickens here.' Then some corn, or some greens, they insisted. 'Nothing, *papay,* there is nothing here.' The travelers went on insisting, and finally asked how people could live there, if they had nothing. The Indian gave them the most marvelous, painful, and profound answer. He said: 'We don't live, *papay,* we endure.'"

39. Document of the Peruvian Episcopal Conference on the Theology of Liberation, October 1984, n. 10.

These ecclesial experiments "have helped the Church to discover the evangelizing potential of the poor" (Puebla 1147).

As the privileged (not exclusive) recipients of the message of the kingdom, the poor are also its bearers. Those ecclesial base communities, which clearly represent one of the most fruitful realities of the Church in Latin America, are one expression of this potential. They stand in the broad stream opened by the Council when it spoke of the People of God and its historic forward movement. They are a manifestation of the People of God in the world of poverty, but they are also — deeply — marked by the Christian faith. They are the ecclesial presence of those deemed insignificant in history, or to use another expression of the Council, of the "messianic people" (LG 9), that is, a people who walk through history, constantly applying the messianic inversion: "the last will be first."

Paschal Service

For the Church to proclaim the Gospel in the heart of the world of poverty means witnessing to life amid the reality of death.

This is done at a cost. That is why Medellín speaks of a "paschal Church." Puebla — after many painful episodes — called it "a servant Church which extends through time the work of Christ, God's Servant, through its diverse ministries and gifts" (n. 1303). The allusion to the suffering servant in this text (Isa. 42 is cited in a note) reveals an awareness of the path the Church must take in its task of service.

In the last analysis, the poverty that is lived in Latin America means a situation of premature and unjust death, from hunger and illness or from the repressive methods used by those who are defending their privileges. Besides physical death there is cultural death from the devaluation of races and cultures and from the refusal to recognize the full dignity of women, especially those in the exploited social sectors.

The answer to that reality of death is to proclaim life: to proclaim the kingdom of life as an expression of God's love for every person. Those who take on this task commit themselves to the liberation of the poor. In the Latin American situation, to liberate means to give life — all of life, because liberation in Christ is integral; liberation from the last roots of injustice in all its forms: including sin, but also whatever keeps a human being from living as such.

In Latin America, the service of the Church to the world of which the Council speaks so eloquently takes the form of witness and proclamation of total liberation in Christ, not as something that can be fully realized in history, but as something that already — amid great difficulty and resistance — breaks the bonds of selfishness and opens up the gift of fellowship and communion. Therefore to speak of liberation does not mean, as some people seem to think, adopting an enthusiastic and facile optimism. On the contrary, the language of liberation can only come from an experience of oppression and death, without which liberation itself has no meaning.

Moreover, as we have so often seen in these times, in Latin America few things are as life-threatening as defending the right to life. The path of commitment to the poorest and most oppressed of the continent is strewn with the imprisonment, torture, disappearance, exile, and death of many people. Many Christians are among them, mistreated precisely because they have witnessed to the Gospel through their efforts of solidarity with the marginalized. Perhaps we are still too close to understand the martyrial reality of the Latin American Church, but it is clear that the Church has been changed by the witness of so many of her children.

The Church of the poor disturbs and injures the interests of the great in this world, whatever their ideological inclination. Thus it also finds the cross of the Lord on this path. This is a paschal Church, in the words of Medellín, and therefore it can never be triumphalistic, as people said in the days of the Council. The blood of those who show their love of God by their solidarity with the poor is proof of that encounter with death and the cross. But "the blood of Christians is like a seed" of new life and hope, as *Ad Gentes* says (5; see also 24).

The blood of martyrs always gives new life to the Church. The

Latin American Christian community is experiencing it today and intends to embrace the free gift of God's love at the same time that it takes up its task with the poorest. This is the community's painful and joyful — paschal — role, which no one can deny it.

Conclusion

The maturity of the Latin American Church is expressed at Medellín by taking the path of the preferential option for the poor — with all its implications for us — in order to be an authentic sign of the kingdom of life. The connection and mutual enrichment of these three elements brings the Latin American Church into full communion with the universal Church.

That was the result of the effort to see the Latin American situation in the light of Vatican II. John XXIII and the Council called for attentiveness to the signs of the times. Medellín responded by seeing — beyond isolated anecdotes — the deep desire for liberation of a people who live in poverty and oppression, but who are at the same time a believing people. The Church offers its solidarity to this people because it knows that in doing so it verifies its faithfulness to Christ, as John Paul II has said (*Laborem Exercens* 8).

The relevance of the poor to the kingdom of God, and therefore to the proclamation of the Gospel, is at the heart of the change that the Latin American Church is experiencing. Only in this context were Medellín and Puebla (and the theology of liberation) able to understand poverty in its social dimensions. The option for the poor is a theocentric option: faith in the God of Jesus Christ is its first and most important basis.

The preferential option for the poor is the way to show the presence of the kingdom of God in Latin American history. We repeat: therein lies the maturity achieved at Medellín by the Church present on this continent. This is the most meaningful aspect of that conference, and its most original contribution to the universal Church which, as Rahner said, began a third period of its historical development at the Council.

This was fully understood at Medellín. The words of Cardinal Landázuri in his often-quoted closing address are revealing:

"There is something very characteristic in the positions we have taken in these days, which I want to emphasize. It is this: we are facing our problems. There is a kind of servitude that is not communion. There is a psychological and sociological dependency that does not respond to an intimate union with the Body of the Lord. To face our problems requires maturity."[40]

Indeed Medellín was about becoming an adult Church, which is the precondition of faithfulness to the Word of life and solidarity with a people who are dying unjustly.

Medellín gave clarity to the question, how should we be the Church? As John XXIII put it, how should we say today in Latin America, "thy kingdom come"? And Medellín gave the beginning of an answer to those questions. The path that was opened at Medellín continued and matured at Puebla; the conference held in 1992 in Santo Domingo will also follow that path. It is the path on which the whole Church proclaims, through the suffering and death of many, its hope in the definitive victory of the life of the Resurrected One.

— *Translated by Margaret Wilde*

---

40. *Signos de Renovación*, 252.

– 4 –

Toward the Fifth Centenary

The year 1992 is more than just a date. It is an occasion to render an account of the last five hundred years which — whether we like it or not — have determined our lives in Latin America to this day and have also been decisive for Europe and other continents. The initial event is called discovery, meeting, conquest by some; cover-up, un-meeting, and invasion by others. In this process the Christian faith has been present — and absent — in various ways. The latter will be particularly taken into account in the Fourth Conference of Latin American Bishops (Santo Domingo, October 1992), which will aim to seek — as they did before at Medellín (1968) and Puebla (1979) — ways of announcing the Gospel for the time to come.

This matter is engaging the attention of many people, coming from different spiritual families. Naturally their focus is different and they may take opposite positions on the historical process and a present reality whose wounds are still raw. It is a matter which primarily concerns those who live in Latin America, who are asking themselves once again in their rather short history what it means to be Latin American. The matter also concerns Europe, whose past as a colonial power still weighs on it, and it has repercussions in Africa, where the population suffered an increase in the inhuman slave trade. The debate revives ancient passions and produces great anger.

Published in *Páginas* 99 (October 1989): 7–17 and *Concilium* 232 (1990): 373–83.

From the History of the Other

We must also have the courage to read the facts from the other side of history. Here our sense of truth is at stake. In fact only historical honesty can free us from prejudices, narrowness, ignorance, fudging by interested parties, which makes our past a burdensome mortgage instead of an impulse to creativity.

Recovering our memory will make us throw out the so-called "black legend" and "rosy legend" as inadequate and therefore useless. Hiding what really happened during those years for fear of the truth in order to defend entrenched privileges or — at the other extreme — frivolously mouthing mere slogans condemns us to historical sterility. Nor does it accord with the demands of the Gospel. This is how the Gospel was understood by many of those who first came to proclaim it to this continent, and therefore they firmly denounced everything that went against the life-affirming will of the God of the kingdom of love and justice. This made the Peruvian Indian Guamán Poma exclaim, reproachfully but also with hope: "And so, my God, where are you? You do not hear me to relieve your poor."[1]

Trying to cover up the witnesses of the time to the immense destruction of persons, peoples, and cultures, together with their vital links with the natural world, is like trying to cover the sun with one hand. Innumerable texts of missionaries (Dominicans, Franciscans, Augustinians, Jesuits, Mercedarians, and many more), members of the indigenous populations, bishops, chroniclers, and historians of the era have left accounts of an atrocious reality — whatever the exact figures — of a demographic collapse.[2] The memory of these events annoys the European nations very much:

---

1. *El primer nueva corónica y buen gobierno* (a work written at the beginning of the seventeenth century). I quote from the Siglo XXI edition (Mexico City, 1980), 1104.

2. In the Pontifical Commission for Justice and Peace document *The Church and Racism* (1988), we read: "The first great wave of European colonization was in fact accompanied by massive destruction of the pre-Columbian civilizations and by the brutal subjection of their inhabitants. Although the great sailors of the fifteenth and sixteenth centuries may have been free from racial prejudices, the soldiers and traders did not practice the same respect. They killed in order to establish themselves; they reduced the 'Indians' to slavery to use them as manpower, as they did later the blacks, and developed a racist theory in order to justify themselves" (3).

Spain and Portugal were present from the beginning and, in the majority, France, England, and Holland a bit later; Germany only partially, Italy and other countries through some of their citizens. These countries are proud of the enterprise which they think of as civilizing and bringing the Gospel.

It is historically false to claim that the evidence is only in documents inspired by Las Casas. Much of it appears earlier than the work of the great defender of the Indians, or comes from persons and areas not under his influence, even some of his enemies, such as the Franciscan Motolinía (a missionary in Mexico). This is an attempt to confine the evidence to the ideas and presumed prejudices of "a single man," as the famous document of Yucay (Cusco, 1571) claims,[3] when actually the facts are attested by numerous witnesses. What these accounts have in common is the situation they witnessed, not a reading of the same texts. This same ploy is used today with the same object: to cover up an unjust and challenging reality.

Perhaps Las Casas went most deeply into what happened at the time and articulated the most thorough theological reflection on these events. But in so doing he was only a *primus inter pares,* because there were many who went long with him and shared his hopes. What he did, together with an important group of friars and bishops — and a little later our Guamán Poma — was to denounce the oppression and death suffered by the inhabitants of the Indias, stating clearly it was caused by greed for gold, which Scripture calls idolatry, as Fray Bartolomé himself points out. These men also declared that the injustices and ill treatment existing before the arrival of the Europeans (facts whose cruelty we must also look squarely in the face) could not in any way legitimize the exploitation and dispossession of the Indians. These are elemental truths rooted in human rights and the Christian message. In stating this these men risked their lives, and Bishop Valdivieso in Nicaragua, for example, actually forfeited his.

These representatives of the best of Spain also risked their rep-

---

3. See on this text G. Gutiérrez, *Dios o el oro en las Indias: Siglo XVI* (Lima: CEP, 1989).

utation because they were considered — and still are by those who are ignorant of the new historical writing on the period — to be holders of extreme positions and enemies of their country. Their sin was unmasking those whose behavior brought shame on their country and made a mockery of the Christian faith they claimed to uphold. Thus in Spain and in the Indias they managed to provoke a discussion on the legitimacy of the European colonial presence and its methods which no other Old World country had the courage to undertake, in spite of their Christian and humanist pretensions. They also left us testimonies of realities that they themselves were trying to change, many of which we would not know about without their work. This was a difficult task in the circumstances of the time. We should appreciate it — with its limits and possibilities — in its historical context, as well as in its later repercussions.

Las Casas left us an important route by which to explore our past today. He told the European theologians (in particular John Major, a Scottish professor in Paris at the beginning of the sixteenth century) who had not set foot in these countries but were justifying the deeds being done in them: "If we were Indian we should see things differently." This is a firm recognition of otherness and a "no" to integration by means of subjection and absorption of the inhabitants of the Indias. It is also a summons, still difficult for many people today, to change our point of view in order to understand these events.

History written from the conqueror's viewpoint has long hidden important aspects of the reality from us. The "other" in Latin America remains "open-veined" — to use the famous expression of the Uruguayan writer Eduardo Galeano — precisely because the poorest of its inhabitants are not recognized in the fullness of their human dignity. Their "distance" from the present socioeconomic order and the dominant culture makes the poor, the other, our neighbor before anyone else, as we have been taught from the outset of liberation theology by the parable of the Good Samaritan.[4]

---

4. See G. Gutiérrez, *A Theology of Liberation,* rev. ed. (Maryknoll, N.Y.: Orbis Books, 1988), 113–15.

The history is largely of the Indians' resistance to the foreign invasion and the contempt for human values that came with it. It was an opposition which in spite of everything managed to preserve cultural traditions and keep alive our languages, which nourish the present and are a vital element in our identity.

One way of recognizing the others' historical roots is to hold penitential celebrations among the quincentenary events (the opening of the Fourth Conference of Latin American Bishops could be an excellent occasion). It is not a question of masochistic posturing, which is ultimately barren and narcissistic. The point is that no one escapes responsibility for what the poor went through and are going through now. The Christian way of assuming this responsibility is humbly to ask forgiveness from God and the victims of history for our complicity — explicit or tacit, in the past and the present, as individuals and as Church — in this situation. Seeking forgiveness means wanting life; it expresses a will to change our behavior and reaffirms our duty to be an effective sign in the history of the kingdom of love and justice.

Not Forgetting the Present

However, it is important to point out that the purpose of looking back at this history is to deal with our present situation and to show solidarity with the poor today. The quincentenary must not become an invitation to turn back the historical clock. Our approach to the past must be motivated not by nostalgia but by hope; not by a fixation upon former painful and traumatic occurrences, but by present suffering and the conviction that only a people which has a memory can transform the situation it is in and build a different world. History, as Bartolomé de Las Casas insisted, "is the teacher of all things," as long as we turn to it in order to understand our own time better. We cannot remain fixed in the past. Thus J. C. Mariátegui called upon us not to get stuck in the past:

> The Conquest, evil and all, was a historical fact. The Republic, such as it exists, is another historical fact. Against

historical facts neither the mind's abstract speculations nor the spirit's highest ideas can do much. The history of Peru is just a piece of human history. Over four centuries a new reality has come about. The input from the West has created it. It is a fragile reality. But at any rate, it is a reality. It would be excessively romantic to decide to ignore it today.[5]

We cannot remake history. It is a matter of realism.

Doubtless this approach has its risks; it must be made with respect for the temporal and cultural coordinates of the past. Impatience to learn from history sometimes leads us to manipulate it, pretending, for example, that conditions and opinions repeat themselves just as they are. These are facile comparisons which do not take the density of history into account and prevent us from looking at present challenges with fresh eyes. So unless we broaden the term excessively, we cannot call certain sixteenth-century missionaries and theologians "liberation theologians" (an expression which has a precise contemporary meaning), as if we were giving them a medal. Saying that someone in the past was brilliant intellectually because he thought in his time as we do today is to allow ourselves to be contaminated by the arrogance of the modern spirit. Modernity considers itself supreme in history, hence its greatest praise for contributions by thinkers in previous eras of humanity is to say "they were ahead of their time." That is, they were "modern" before their time.

For example, calling Las Casas a liberation theologian can of course draw attention to certain aspects of his thinking, but it unwittingly obscures others. So we think such a title neither appropriate nor necessary to appreciate his thought and testimony. He lived in a context very different from our own; both at the social and the theological level the language is also different. Its depth comes from its Gospel roots and from the way in which Las Casas keeps faith with his Lord. Approaching this witness to God's love on our continent means respecting him in his world, in his time, and with his sources, and being clear about his limitations. This

---

5. *Peruanicemos al Perú* (Lima: Amauta, 1970), 66.

attitude does not distance us from his work but brings us closer, without trying to abuse it to serve our present way of defending causes, which indeed have the same root. Therefore we must be able to confront new challenges in our own way, while at the same time we must learn from men like Pedro de Córdoba, Juan de Zumárraga, Vasco de Quiroga, Juan del Valle, Guamán Poma, and so many others who lived and worked in these lands.

Our interest and our protest at what happened in the sixteenth century to the different Indian nations and cultures should not make us overlook the events of the centuries that came afterward with the arrival of new races and cultures, or the exploitation and dispossession of the poor on our continent today. It would be very wrong if the quincentenary confined us to the sixteenth century.

Today among the poor, as José María Arguedas puts it, "all bloods" are represented. This creates a very different state of affairs from that confronting the Indians — and those in solidarity with them — in the past. But their testimony has much to teach us about how to respond to the challenges and social conflicts of our own time. Today too there is destruction of people and cultures, and we go on hearing "the just cries which have universally risen to heaven," as Tupac Amaru II said in eighteenth-century Peru, when he rebelled against the colonial order.

In Latin America, to contrast, as some have begun to do, the Indian with the poor is a subtle form of remaining anchored in the past, even though claiming to adopt a new position. We can only be glad that these people are now discovering those who are marginalized in our society, because for so long they were unconcerned about them except as objects of study. Criticism of what is unilateral and squalid in certain current social analyses which ignore the racial question is valid and should be retained. But we should not separate aspects that mutually imply one another and, precisely because they do not fuse, concur to show us the complexity of the world of the poor, dispossessed, and despised. This is an enrichment which we must keep. Making our task easier by picking and choosing when it is not possible to do so takes us away from the real people, their social and cultural universe, as well as from their sufferings, claims, and hopes today.

It is urgent that we should build a society in accordance with the interests and values of the poor today, social classes and races and cultures that are dispossessed and marginalized, women, and especially those who belong to these sectors of society. The great cultural and ethnic variety of Latin America must be welcomed without trying to impose a single cultural form, the Western, which arrived very late, as *the* culture of the region. To claim that Western culture brings the Gospel is to ignore the Church's experience of Pentecost. According to the Acts of the Apostles the miracle of Pentecost did not consist in speaking a single language; rather, those who had come from different racial and cultural areas heard the apostles speaking "each in *his own language.*" This was not uniformity, but dialogue and unity based on respect for difference. It was not imposed integration, but acceptance of otherness and ethnic and cultural heterogeneity. The process designated by the neologism "inculturation" is highly necessary. For a Christian it also has resonances of incarnation, and therefore of authentic and profound presence in history. So concern for our present situation cannot be absent in our approach to our past. In the history of today, Christians decide on their discipleship and solidarity with the poor and oppressed.

With Boldness

Reading history from the other side and in the light of our current concerns means seeking truth and solidarity. We must also add a perspective of future and of hope.

The present acquires density when it is nourished by the memory of a journey, when it has the courage to identify the problems that have not been solved and that therefore need great efforts now. This is what is happening in Latin America with the racial question. As we know, one of our great social lies is saying that there is no racism on this continent. Of course we do not have racist laws. But given the small weight of the law among us, this has little significance. However, we have something much worse and much more difficult to eradicate: entrenched racist customs. Anything coming from an Indian, black, or Amazonian background is an object of frivolous interest and, with important exceptions, is despised and marginalized. "They made you an anonymous collective without face or history," as the poet-bishop Pedro Casaldáliga expressively puts it, speaking of those who have felt this disdain and "blanking" for centuries. Racism is undoubtedly an important component in the diverse and cruel situation of violence (institutional, terrorist, repressive) experienced today in Latin America.

We have to take the present as we find it and deal with the situation as it is and not as we might wish it to be. We have to deal with the unfinished process of nonmeetings and forced meetings between races and cultures, in the present poverty and injustice suffered by the majorities. We must also be clear who are the agents in the liberating force at work among us. It is too complex to oversimplify into separate Hispanic and indigenous trends.

This is a society in the process of becoming. Its ancient wounds still have not healed, and it has trampled peoples and cultures underfoot. And even today most of its members suffer poverty and dispossession as they struggle to affirm their dignity as persons. In this society the Church is called to a "new way of preaching the Gospel," to which it has been committed since Medellín.[6] This call has been taken up with vigor and clarity by John Paul II in the perspective of the quincentenary.[7] But this new preaching still requires the testimony of the great Gospel preachers of the past. They were great defenders of the Indians, nor could they fail to be. We have already noted that this produces disagreement among us, and it also did in their time. That is inevitable. To speak from the standpoint of the poor, with them and not just for them, always means threatening privileged interests, as long as the enormous unjust inequalities and oppression exist.

The new Gospel-preaching will have to address the challenges with which the past and present history of the continent present it.

---

6. See the message of the conference (and also the preparatory document).
7. Speech in Haiti (October 1983). In fact the pope had already used the expression "new Gospel-preaching" in Poland (speech in the city of Nova Huta, June 9, 1981). See Cecilia Tovar, "Juan Pablo II y la nueva evangelización," in *Páginas* 102 (April 1990): 35–54.

The discussion that arose around Medellín became sharper round Puebla, and it gains new urgency as we approach the fourth conference of Latin American bishops. Once again the debate will be fruitful, always supposing, of course, that it takes on the new conditions, challenges, and reflections. Latin America is too large and diverse to be explained by summary analyses.

We have to overcome the temptation — through exhaustion, fear, or interest — to overlook the real challenges from a cruel, complex, and painful reality. The Church must listen to all the voices trying to make themselves heard in Latin America. It is an excellent opportunity to survey the whole of that history bursting upon us today. Not everything in the present is synthesis and soil waiting for the seed of the Gospel, only threatened by recent and alien ideas connected with modern society, as some people seem to think. Contemporary factors as well as a disputed history play their part. Culture is permanent creativity. It cannot be defended as tradition if it is not at the same time thrusting forward. The daily life of the poor is, in spite of everything, a permanent source of hope. It ensures that joy does not vanish. For the prophet Joel (1:12), the absence of joy was the major sign of the deep crisis afflicting his nation.

The presence of the Church in this process has its "lights and shadows," as Medellín said. But over these last two decades, the experiences, reflections, and testimonies of many Christians constitute a great richness with which to face our task. The new Gospel-preaching to the continent began during these years. They have seen the development of a Church able to confront the reality in which it has to announce the Gospel message, and a new way of being Christian. Both these must continue to grow. The resistance and ignorance to be found today in some Church circles is a cause for concern because they are opposing the most fruitful recent tendencies in pastoral work and theology in Latin America.

We do not want merely to repeat what has been discovered or done during this time. We should avoid confusing radicalness with intellectual laziness and lack of determination to innovate and learn. A great creative force is necessary to confront the present challenges. What has been done in Latin America, for example in theology, during these decades must be rethought and reformulated, incorporating other themes and perspectives. Faithfulness to the God of our faith and to the poor implies a permanent tension between the Gospel and walking with a people who are living in a changing situation.

In all this there are obvious successes, but there are still many more things that remain to be done and to change, including those within the Church. Therefore Puebla calls all Christians and the Church as a whole to conversion. This cannot be achieved without an attitude that the Acts of the Apostles at the dawn of missionary work in the Christian community calls *parrhesia*. This Greek term means boldness, outspokenness, the opposite of the timidity we see at present in so many Church circles. There is no other way to preach the Gospel. The times call us to confront the present challenges with *parrhesia*. This is based on hope in the Lord who is the truth, who — according to Las Casas — "has a very vivid memory of the most forgotten and the littlest" and "makes everything new" (Rev. 21:1). This newness will also affect our Latin American identity and our way of proclaiming — amid a reality marked by untimely and unjust death — the kingdom of life.

— Translated by Dinah Livingstone

– 5 –

An Agenda
The Conference at Santo Domingo

The road to the final document of the fourth Latin American episcopal conference in Santo Domingo was marked by long preparation, high expectations, more than a few tensions, fearfulness on many sides, old suspicions, the power and presence of an ecclesial itinerary, last-minute maneuvers, serenity and pastoral discernment on the part of many participants, the growing poverty of the Latin American people, and a lot of praying.

The days of the conference itself were equally dense and complex. A rather confusing system of work and other factors made it impossible to produce a document with the same theological scope as those of previous episcopal conferences. But that was not the goal of this conference. At several points the text simply refers back to the doctrinal framework and basic options established at those assemblies. Thus the earlier conference documents are key to the interpretation of this one.[1] From this perspective, Santo Domingo (hereafter SD) gives important explanations and — in a persuasive tone, without anathematizing other viewpoints — presents relevant points of the agenda of commitment and reflection that Christians on the continent had opened in those years.

Published in *Páginas* 119 (February 1993) and in *Santo Domingo: Ensaios Teologico-Pastorais* (Petrópolis: Vozes, 1993), 55–68). The Santo Domingo documents cited here are reprinted in Alfred T. Hennelly, ed., *Santo Domingo and Beyond* (Maryknoll, N.Y.: Orbis Books, 1993).

1. There are few explicit citations of the texts of Medellín and Puebla, but the document often refers to the messages of those assemblies and clearly affirms its continuity with them.

There will be plenty of reports to fill in the stages of the preparatory process, and plenty of observers will describe the vicissitudes and tensions experienced during this episcopal conference. That is needed in order to understand the document. But our emphasis in these pages will be on the core of the document, on the tasks that lie ahead. The challenges are great and will require all our energy.

An Option and Three Pastoral Lines

From the beginning of the preparation to the conference itself, the perspective was that of the new evangelization which was affirmed at Medellín and has since been energetically picked up by John Paul II.

One of the first documents of the preparatory stage presented, and juxtaposed, two great challenges to the proclamation of the Gospel in Latin America. Some people said that the more important of these challenges came from the modern culture, the "new culture," in the expression used at Puebla.[2] Others affirmed that the more important challenge was the terrible poverty prevailing in Latin America, and even added that "the precondition for the new evangelization is the preferential option of solidarity with the poor."

As the theme developed, the relationship between modernity and poverty became clearer, and with it the need to deal with the diverse challenges to evangelization together. This task must begin with the situation of misery and marginalization experienced by the majority of the Latin American population. That approach was promoted in comments and critiques on the preparatory document and more decisively in the contributions of the various episcopates.[3]

Those contributions were summarized in the document called "Segunda relatio," a key text on the way to Santo Domingo (diligently prepared by Angel Salvatierra, whose premature death is

---

2. This expression appears only once in SD (see n. 30).
3. These have been published by CELAM: *Aportes de las Conferencias Episcopales a la IV Conferencia* (Bogotá, 1992).

mourned by all his friends). That text was the basis of the "Working document" (hereafter, WD) which laid the basis for the work of the conference and which would have been very useful in editing its texts. At one key point, however, the final document explains and improves several potentially confusing terms in the WD. We are referring to the range of options which the WD offers the Latin American Church under the rubric of "preferential options."[4] In addition to the option for the poor, they include the options for youth (already present at Puebla), for the family, for the laity, for the evangelization of modern culture, and several others. Santo Domingo did not follow that line, but rightly distinguished between the preferential option for the poor and other pastoral priorities.[5]

We are not quibbling over words here, nor devaluing the other pastoral challenges that come from our reality. What was at stake (although not everyone saw it at first) was the need to keep clear the evangelical perspective which has inspired the pastoral action of the Latin American Church for the past twenty-five years, and which has since been echoed at the universal level. That clarity is required, not for our own intellectual satisfaction, but for the fruitfulness of the pastoral lines to be adopted; the axis on which they turn gives those pastoral lines greater scope.

Santo Domingo solidly reaffirms the preferential option for the poor. In the christological perspective that marks the conference, according to its assigned theme: "Jesus Christ yesterday, today, and forever" (Heb. 13:8),[6] this option is based on Christ and his proclamation of the Good News to the poor (see Luke 4:18–19). SD says: "Such is the basis for our commitment to a Gospel-based and preferential option for the poor, one that is firm and irrevocable but not exclusive or excluding, as was very solemnly affirmed

---

4. We must observe, however, that in the development of this paragraph only the option for the poor is described as a "preferential option"; the others are simply called options.

5. See observations on this point in the articles published in *Páginas* 117 (September 1992), devoted to the Fourth Episcopal Conference.

6. See the important work of C. I. González, *Jesucristo ayer, hoy y siempre* (Bogotá: CELAM, 1991), and M. Diaz Mateos, "Jesucristo ayer, hoy y siempre," in *Páginas* 117 (September 1992): 58–71.

at the Medellín and Puebla Conferences" (178; see also the Message of the Conference, 17). Thus it upholds a clear continuity with Medellín and Puebla, which also carefully sought to establish the roots of the option for the poor in the witness of Jesus.

The following numbers (179 and 180), and many others (see 50, 275, 296, 302), emphasize the centrality of this option and its stamp on the diverse tasks of the Church. Considering the resistance provoked inside and outside the Church by this perspective, its proclamation, and even the terms in which it is expressed (the word "option," for instance), this is clearly a definitive change.

It is at once an old perspective and a new one. Prophetically recalled by John XXIII on the eve of the Council, in recent years it has emerged from the Christian communities' historical commitment and direct contact with the Bible and from their theological reflection on those experiences. It broke forth at Medellín, its terms and concepts were sharpened after that conference, and it appeared in all its maturity at Puebla. John Paul II brought the preferential option for the poor firmly into the ordinary universal magisterium of the Church.[7]

In this way, what has arisen recently as Latin American Christians gradually discovered the biblical meaning of commitment to the poor and their liberation has spread throughout the life of the Church and the continent. That focus has brought the Gospel resoundingly into spaces that were closed to it before; it has given vitality and creativity to many pastoral initiatives; it has stimulated theological reflection in unheard-of directions; it has been stamped by the witness of martyrs and by the modest, everyday commitment of many people;[8] it has caused sufferings whose depth only the Lord knows, and it has also awakened hopes that deepened the people's faithfulness to Jesus and his Church. This

---

7. Obviously the pope's repeated use of the term, especially in the opening address at the Fourth Conference, is one of the reasons for its presence in the texts of the episcopal assembly. John Paul II said, significantly: "In continuity with the Medellín and Puebla conferences, the Church reaffirms the preferential option on behalf of the poor" (16).

8. We regret that SD was not clearer about the painful — but perhaps hopeful — richness that the martyrdom of some of her children has brought to the Latin American Church (but see the reference to them in SD 21).

is surely the most important contribution that the Latin American ecclesial community has made to the universal Church.

The fact that in Santo Domingo the preferential option for the poor was set out as a postulate for ecclesial action only reaffirms the rightness of its insight and the solidity of its agenda. But we must not be content with declarations and texts. These are important, as the documents of Medellín and Puebla show, only if they are incarnated in the life of the Church. There is always a danger that such proclamations will remain as mere words or gestures toward the common people.

The perspective must be carried out in concrete pastoral action. Santo Domingo proposes such action in terms of the great themes assigned to it: new evangelization, human promotion, and inculturated evangelization. The first of these underlines the role of lay people (especially youth) in the evangelizing task, which is the celebration of the faith; it also gives importance to the missionary task of the Latin American Church beyond our continent. We are convinced that the latter is one of the most fruitful paths ahead of us. Along this line, Puebla called us to "give of our poverty" (368); we hope that this will truly be done in the pastoral action of the future (see SD 293–95; see also 12 and 57 on the missionary dimension).

The second great pastoral line is human promotion. Here the accent is on hearing the cry of the poor and on the need to assume "with renewed ardor the evangelical and preferential option for the poor," which "will, in imitation of Jesus Christ, shed light on all our evangelizing activity." SD also declares that "all human life is sacred," and that this should inspire a defense of life and of the family (see 296–97).[9]

The third line refers to the need for inculturated evangelization. Certainly the inculturation of the Gospel is one of the most salient points of Santo Domingo. This is a new term, although the idea is related to the older concept of incarnation. But as we are now being reminded by the commemoration of the first evangelization in Latin America, it is not easy for the Church to separate

---

9. We shall return to some points of the chapter devoted to human promotion.

Western culture from its proclamation of the Gospel. For this reason SD calls on the Church to "undergo a pastoral conversion" (30; see also 23). There is much to do in this area; one fundamental step is to recognize the values of black and indigenous peoples. Another is to accept the challenges of the accelerated process of urbanization and the aggressive presence of the mass communication media in this continent (see 298–301).

The New Faces of Poverty

Santo Domingo takes note of a massive and obvious reality: the growing impoverishment of the majority in Latin America. The cry of the poor which Medellín heard, and which Puebla called "clear, growing, forceful, and sometimes threatening" (89), today has become deafening. Santo Domingo affirms that the poverty "in which millions of our brothers and sisters are plunged — to the point where it is reaching intolerable extremes of misery — is the cruelest and most crushing scourge that Latin America and the Caribbean are enduring" (179).[10] This is one more reason for a preferential option for the poor.

For all these reasons the text invites us "to extend the list of suffering faces" (179) of which Puebla spoke (31–39), in a beautiful passage written by two great Latin American bishops who are no longer with us: Germán Schmitz and Leonidas Proaño. In those faces we must find the features of the Lord,[11] for they challenge us to "a deep personal and ecclesial conversion" (178). They are faces "emaciated by hunger as a result of inflation, foreign debt, and social injustice" (ibid.).[12]

Throughout the document, specific social sectors give a more precise color and shape to the faces of the poor in Latin America. At the time of the conference special attention was being given to the indigenous peoples and the black population (which SD prefers to call Afro-Americans) of the continent. This is an occa-

---

10. The location of the conference on a Caribbean island led to more exact expression: the text always speaks of Latin America and the Caribbean.
11. SD specifically mentions Matthew 25:31–46, to which Puebla refers tacitly.
12. The text follows with examples of those faces.

sion for recognizing the values and appreciating the contribution to Latin American history of these persons and peoples.

As we know, it was not easy to establish the necessary consensus to respond to a longstanding request — that the conference ask forgiveness of the indigenous and black peoples for the participation of Christians in the oppression and injustice to which they were subjected during and after the sixteenth century. SD did so (see 20 and 246), although without the clear intervention of the pope it might not have happened. Several voices expressed resistance to the recognition of events whose historical veracity are not in doubt.[13] Fortunately those obstacles were overcome, but much still remains to be done in solidarity with the indigenous and black people and cultures of Latin America. This is a key element of the agenda that lies ahead.

But the poor are not only marked by their color and often their own language; the condition of women — especially those of the popular sectors — is also an important feature of the situation. In a well-known text, Puebla speaks of women as "doubly oppressed and marginalized" (1134, note) and devotes several paragraphs to the problem (104–10); it denounces the physical abuse of women and the persistent mentality that marginalizes them in the society and in the Church. This is an important point, but it would have been good to say more about organizations formed by women "to demand the respect for their rights" of which Puebla spoke (836). Women certainly comprise one of the most dynamic and creative sectors in the Latin American society and Church. The document

---

13. In the pope's message to the Afro-Americans (October 13), there is a clear recognition of injustice against "the black populations of the African continent" and a request for forgiveness for Christian participation in that abuse. John Paul II had already done the same on the island of Gorea (Africa) in February 1992. The conference participants were less willing to use the same language toward indigenous peoples; in this case, given the massiveness of the event, the implied questioning of the colonial system, and the emotions it aroused, the issue was more controversial. But on October 21, back in Rome, the pope spoke of his trip to Santo Domingo as "an act of expiation" for "the sin, the injustice, and the violence" that accompanied the arrival of Christians in these lands. This led him to a "request for forgiveness, addressed especially to the first inhabitants of the new land, to the Indians, and also to those who were deported there as slaves from Africa to carry out the hardest labors." The most recalcitrant members of the conference were obliged to back down after that statement.

rightly speaks of the need to "delve more deeply into women's role" in both sectors (105). We hope it will happen.[14]

These are all points which need to be more deeply explored. That is not our purpose here; for now we will simply observe the importance of saying that the features of indigenous people, blacks, and women more precisely define the face of the poor in Latin America, in whom we recognize the face of Christ himself. This evangelical perspective, present from the first light of the Latin American reflection on liberation in Christ, not only remains present but has been reinforced by the current situation. To this perspective we owe some of the most fruitful commitments of our time.

Signs of the Times

In recent years the Christian communities of Latin America, and the theological reflection that accompanies them, have opened new themes and have taken some old concerns in unheard-of directions. They grow out of the course of historical events and appear as true signs of the times, signs which must be perceived in order to proclaim the Gospel, and whose call to commitment demands to be heard.

Santo Domingo echoed some of these realities, which open new paths for historical solidarity — especially with the poorest people — and for an intelligent understanding of the faith. By focusing on them we hope to overcome the separation between faith and life to which Santo Domingo often refers (for example, 24, 44, 48). Santo Domingo enumerates some of these "new signs of the times in the area of human promotion." But we also find them in other sections of the document. The central theme of the preferential option for the poor appears forcefully in all these cases. Let us take some examples from that list.

One of the most serious problems of Latin America in recent decades has been, and is, the violation of human rights. It

---

14. The draft text of the commission on women contained important elements which were not included in the summary presented by the final text.

has also been a leading, and dangerous, area of commitment for many Christians and for some churches as institutional bodies. This theme was already present at Puebla (see the document "Dignidad humana"), but it is explored in more detail in SD. Although SD sometimes reflects the fear of some people that this issue might be manipulated (see 168), it rightly explains that human rights are also violated by the poverty and injustice that exist in Latin America (see 167).

Ecology is a great concern of humanity today. It emerged, understandably, in the rich and industrialized countries. Nevertheless it would be a serious error to consider it an artificial concern in the poor countries. For this reason SD attempts to read the problem from the viewpoint of "the world's great impoverished majorities" (169). Indeed, they are often the victims of the development of the large countries. Thus SD calls for "an ecological ethic" which "entails abandoning a utilitarian and individualistic morality." For this purpose it invokes a principle which we believe will prove fruitful in the future: "that the goods of creation are destined for all" (ibid.).

In the same vein it recalls the meaning of land in the gift of creation. This issue is particularly important to the peasants, many of whom also belong to indigenous peoples. They have a religious vision of the "mother earth" which nourishes them. This is in opposition to "the commercial vision [which] looks at the land exclusively in terms of exploitation and profit," and worse, "goes so far as to drive off and forcefully expel its legitimate owners" (172). The latter is a process that began five centuries ago and still has not been resolved. Thus the poverty of the peasants has clear and identifiable causes.

After a long and painful period accompanied by great suffering, the Latin American countries have turned toward democratic governments. Only under these conditions can we begin to build a just and pluralistic society. In several of our nations the Church has played an important role in the process of democratization (see 190).[15] SD realistically acknowledges that the exercise of democ-

---

15. The text shows this in the part that theoretically corresponds to theological en-

racy "is still more formal than real" (191). It also points out that
the democratic order will be established only when the people
achieving it have "real participation" in Latin America (see 191
and 193).

A fundamental condition of authentic respect for human rights
and a democratic organization of society is the establishment of
social justice. Santo Domingo directly addresses what is most controversial on the continent today: economic neoliberalism. This
is one of the most important points in SD. Against "impoverishment and the accentuation of the gap between rich and poor"
(199), it urges us to "lay the groundwork for a real and efficient
economy of solidarity" (201). Such an economy should control
"those mechanisms of the market economy that do deep damage
to the poor" (202). Thus, following the steps of John Paul II, it
denounces the mortgage laid by the external debt on the development of our countries and affirms that the debt cannot be paid at
the cost of the lives of the poorest people (see 197).

Although it is not discussed as a sign of the times, it is important to mention the challenge (among others, naturally) that comes
from the process of urbanization that is occurring in Latin America. This theme was touched on at Medellín and discussed directly
at Puebla. Santo Domingo picks it up, pointing out that it represents a deep cultural change. It is also a situation that increases the
poverty and misery of the majority of the population in the cities,
"the result of exploitive and exclusivist economic models" (255).

•

We have pointed out some of the challenges to the proclamation
of "the Gospel of justice, love and mercy" (13).[16] They all express
aspects of the situation of the poor, the immense majority of the
continent, and call for solidarity with those who suffer marginalization and injustice. "All evangelization must therefore mean

---

lightenment; real-life situations are often found at the beginning of the theological
subjects under discussion. It is hard to object to this traditional — and logical — order.

16. The text approved at Santo Domingo said only "Gospel of justice." The addition is one of the few changes coming out of its revision in Rome. In another,
similar change the document spoke of "the Gospel of human rights"; it now reads "the
Gospel — the deep root of human rights" (165).

inculturating the Gospel," says SD in its profession of faith (13). This process not only involves the old cultures of the continent, but must also take into account the challenges listed here. The Gospel must be inculturated in them. Indeed, this effort "is an imperative of following Jesus and it is necessary in order to restore the disfigured countenance of the world" (13). That is, its goal "will always be the salvation and integral liberation of a particular people or human group" (243).[17] It defends these against "the overwhelming power of the structures of sin manifested in modern society" (ibid.).[18]

In the doctrinal and pastoral context of Medellín and Puebla, without either the prophetic energy of the first or the theological density of the second, Santo Domingo brings together several points of the agenda that Latin American Christians have begun to establish in recent years. The new challenges are well defined; the fruitfulness of the response will depend — as it did in the earlier Latin American episcopal conferences — on our understanding of the texts of Santo Domingo. If we hear its call, we will put an end to useless infighting and move forward in solidarity with all who live on this continent, especially with the poor and oppressed, and gain in ecclesial communion. In that way we will embrace the free gift of the kingdom, in the history of the sufferings and hopes of the Latin American people.

— Translated by Margaret Wilde

---

17. The idea of total or integral liberation is present from the beginning in Latin American theology, Medellín, and Puebla, which distinguish three levels within it: liberation from unjust structures, liberation of the human person, and liberation from sin. This last dimension is considered in SD as a synonym of reconciliation (see 123), which leaves no room for facile opposition. Indeed reconciliation, like liberation, is an old and traditional Christian idea which no one can claim as private property.

18. This perspective was adopted — not without difficulty — long ago in Latin America; it led to the description of the continental reality as a "situation of sin" (Medellín, "Peace" 1). The biblical roots of this approach are clear; that explains its presence in the universal magisterium of the Church as well.

– 6 –

Liberation and Development

A Challenge to Theology

The theme of our seminar is "Liberation and Development." These are key points for an understanding of the Latin American reality; the relationship between them has led to many studies and more than a few controversies.

To propose one or the other — or both — as ways out of the poverty and injustice experienced in Latin America assumes an understanding of that situation and a way of analyzing it. We are not speaking of something abstract; this state of affairs conditions the everyday life of the Latin American people and sets the direction we must take in solidarity with the poor in order to build a world of justice for all. This reality also frames the evangelizing task of the Church. Indeed, the Gospel is addressed to real people: their historical situation presents us with specific challenges which we cannot ignore and which stimulate our understanding of the faith. The theology of liberation grows out of these interwoven elements.

For this reason we are especially interested in the changes that are occurring in the social sphere and, therefore, in our way of understanding them. That is what has been happening to us in recent years. Over the years our realities and perspectives have undergone changes, sometimes radical ones. Our categories and reference points cannot remain the same. We have a compelling

Presentation at the seminar "Liberación y desarrollo en América Latina: Perspectivas," organized by the Instituto Bartolomé de Las Casas (June 1992), published in the book by the same title (Lima: CEP-IBC, 1993), and in *Páginas* 124 (December 1993): 14–23.

need for a perspective that is at once evaluative and prospective. This seminar, set in the context of the social disciplines, seeks to contribute to that task. For this reason we saw the need to invite seasoned veterans of these struggles as well as younger researchers.

My task is not to intervene in the specialized areas under discussion, but to say a few brief words about the influence of the social sciences among Christians who in recent years have found the faith — and reflection on it — to be a source of inspiration for their commitment to the poor and oppressed of the continent. To make this solidarity effective we need an adequate understanding of the economic and social reality of Latin America.

The Challenge of Poverty

One clear and decisive event has occurred in the recent life of the Latin American Church: its conception of the task of proclaiming the Gospel has been changed by a new awareness of the "inhuman misery" (Medellín, "Poverty" 1) in which the immense majority of the population live. Poverty remains the great challenge to Christian witness on our continent; before and after Puebla, all efforts to draw attention away from that situation toward other questions have been in vain. Reality and evangelical necessities have conspired to close off all avenues of escape.

Thus theological reflection also cannot stay the same. It has followed unfamiliar paths which — though not without difficulties and misunderstandings — have opened fruitful possibilities for the proclamation of the kingdom of God, as we have seen in these years.

The Presence of the Absent Ones

Christian participation in the process of liberation in Latin America, which we have just called the greatest event in the life of the Church, is only one expression of the vast historical process we know as the irruption of the poor. This situation has shown us with uncommon force and clarity the anguish and cruel poverty of the great majority of the Latin American population, which has entered the social scene — as Las Casas said of the Indian nations of his time — with "their poverty on their backs." But this situation has also helped us to appreciate the energies and the values of the poor.

Thus our time is marked by a new presence of the poor, the marginalized, and the oppressed. Those who were long "absent" in our society and in the Church have become — are becoming today — present. We are not speaking of a physical absence; these are people whose lives had little or no meaning and who therefore did not feel (in many cases still do not feel) able to express their suffering, their purpose, and their hopes. That is what has begun to change.

It is always difficult to put a date on the beginning of historical processes; the dates are often established approximately and by convention. We can say, however, that the process began thirty or forty years ago. It first appeared in events like a growing popular movement, an intensification of the struggle for justice, a rise in expectations, new social and political organizations, a greater awareness of the personal dignity and rights of the ancient indigenous peoples, efforts by the powerful to carry out relevant social reforms, and even — in some cases — outbreaks of guerrilla violence. All this brought as a reaction a new type of authoritarian and repressive government within the context of the cold war.

These events are complex, sometimes ambiguous or disgraceful, and the forms they take have changed over the last couple of decades. But they represent a challenge with many promising aspects; the poor have begun to see themselves as the subject of their own history and have begun to take their destiny into their own hands. This is an important discovery and a deep conviction, pregnant with social and pastoral consequences. We are seeing the development of what people now call self-esteem, and with it the appearance of new social actors. All this has had a decisive influence on political activity in the Latin American society, and also on the action of the Church.

The challenge for the evangelizing task is further sharpened when we consider that the people who are erupting on the historical landscape are both a poor and a Christian people. The Christian faith marks their way of living poverty and oppression, while poverty and oppression mark their way of experiencing the Gospel.

Poverty and Theological Reflection

These events have revived and redirected the theme of poverty in the universal Church since the middle of this century. We are referring to the demand for an authentic and radical witness of poverty that has emerged in new religious communities, whose members are concerned with alienation from the faith in the world of labor, in social doctrine, and in certain spiritual and pastoral trends. This concern was urgently and prophetically expressed in the famous challenge of John XXIII to the Council: to be the Church for all, and especially the Church of the poor (September 11, 1962).

For well-known and easily understood reasons, Vatican II did not respond adequately to Pope John's proposal, although it was insistently repeated during the work of the Council. But it was heard, with some vacillation and mistrust at first, in the predominantly poor and Christian continent that is Latin America. Together with the new presence of the poor, the vision of a Church of the poor stimulated new theological reflection.

Thus around July 1967 there emerged a distinction among three meanings of the word "poverty": real (or material) poverty as an evil, spiritual poverty as childlike trust, and poverty as solidarity with the poor and as a protest against their situation. This approach entails some analysis of poverty and its causes; it requires a biblical basis, both for the rejection of this inhuman situation and for our understanding of spiritual poverty; and finally, it explains the reasons — beyond idealism — for Christian commitment in this area.

This distinction was picked up a year later at Medellín (1968) and gave new clarity to the commitment that many people were beginning to make. Between Medellín and Puebla (1979) the distinction led to a new expression: "preferential (spiritual poverty) option (poverty as solidarity and protest) for the poor (those who suffer real poverty)." This option has become the axis on which the pastoral action of the Church turns and an important model for Christian life. It shows the meaning of what we call spirituality, the dominant and motivating concern of liberation theology. As you know, it has now been fully accepted as part of the magisterium of the universal Church.

The theme of liberation is closely linked to that of poverty caused by injustice; liberation in turn brings together several approaches. The word has a social and political meaning but also comes from a long biblical and theological tradition. From the beginning it was used to denote the creative development of human abilities in the economic and social spheres, but it also included personal dimensions and a change of attitudes toward the organization of society.

Theologically it means liberation from selfishness and sin, which are understood in the light of faith as the ultimate roots of the injustice that must be eliminated; by overcoming sin we open the way for renewed friendship with God and other people. Separately and together, these dimensions reflect an integral, radical reality: a broad process which takes its ultimate meaning from salvation in Christ. Thus the concept of liberation is now seen as a timeless and challenging summons.

This approach has become the cornerstone of the evangelizing mission of the Latin American Church in our time. It combines a deep sense of God's free gift of love and the urgent need for solidarity with those who historically come in last. A theological process of several decades is beautifully and concisely expressed in the metaphor of encountering the Lord in the suffering faces of the dispossessed and devalued people of our continent — a metaphor drawn from early theological reflection in Latin America on the Gospel of Matthew and later taken up by the conferences at Puebla and Santo Domingo.

Theology and the Social Sciences

The irruption of the poor in the social sphere has led to a process different from the one we have been describing. These began as parallel movements which subsequently crossed paths and enriched each other, but each of which has maintained its own dynamic.

A New Social Awareness

For a long time we Latin Americans have lived in great ignorance about the reality of our nations. In the past, isolated voices — some of them even speaking with authority — alerted us to the problems created by great social separation, but they were silenced by indifference and insensitivity to the marginalization of the poor. In the 1950s several factors led to concern for what was then being called economic and social development. Beginning with the conference at Bandung (1955), those terms were used to express the aspirations of neglected peoples for more human living conditions. Developmentist policies were applied in Latin America with the goal of rescuing our countries from their helplessness. But the optimism surrounding those policies soon dried up.

In response to developmentism — not to development, which is a technical concept and a need for all peoples — there emerged a theory of dependency. Its first elements were defined in the neostructuralist circles of CEPAL (the United Nations Economic Council on Latin America). This approach gradually gained currency with contributions from different sectors of the social sciences and political thought, with and without the influence of Marxist analysis. Unlike developmentism, dependency theory is based on an in-depth study of the causes of Latin American poverty and places it in an international context. Significantly, it also exposes the trajectory that has led to this state of affairs, insisting that each nation lives in an increasingly universal history. Thus the fundamental demand of this approach is to find ways to break away from their dependency on the great centers of power.

These two aspects of dependency theory — its identification of the reasons for poverty and its goal of breaking dependency — made it similar to the approach we have just described, inspired by new sensitivity to the situation of the Latin American majority and by the pastoral and spiritual response to that situation. Thus the theory of dependency, which was prevalent in the 1960s and '70s, became a key instrument for understanding Latin American social and economic reality. It encouraged a structural analysis of the present evils and suggested ways of remedying them.

This theory clearly represented a qualitative difference in our understanding of Latin American reality. Its presence in the framework of liberation theology and in the Medellín documents must be understood exclusively in the context of social analysis. It became an instrument for the understanding of the particular aspect of reality that it addresses. Its contribution was significant in the early years of theological reflection in Latin America. That fact is clear and well known. But as always in the history of theology, the understanding of faith is not identical with the intellectual path used to approach one dimension of human existence. This does not mean that as the challenges of faith are better understood, the use of that path will not lead to priorities that influence reflection on ways of transforming reality, in this case through the task of evangelization. It is necessary to make these links and differences clear.

Like all theories, dependency theory is called to move forward and change as the situations it seeks to explain undergo change. Indeed the instruments of social analysis do change with the passage of time, according to their ability to understand the phenomena on which they are reporting and according to the effectiveness of the solutions they propose. Therefore the proper role of science is to criticize its assumptions and the results it obtains; scientific understanding always moves forward by means of new interpretive hypotheses.

Several prudent studies have recently been devoted to a critical evaluation of dependency theory. Many people today — without devaluing its usefulness at a given time — no longer consider it an effective way of explaining present reality; even in retrospect we are more aware of its inherent limitations (for example, its overemphasis on the external causes of underdevelopment). That is normal, and always happens with attempts to study a shifting terrain. Similar cases have occurred in other social and psychological sciences. The passage of time is merciless toward these efforts at understanding.

It would be wrong either to discount the contribution of this theory or to fail to acknowledge its shortcomings. But it would be even worse to cling doggedly to a tool that obviously no longer responds adequately to the complexity of reality or to the changes that have occurred in that reality. Many of these come from important changes in the international context; others from diverse perceptions of elements which, although they have long been a part of the Latin American social framework, are more clearly and forcefully visible today.

The Present Situation

The first thing to remember in the present state of affairs is that poverty has cruelly increased. The gap between the richest and poorest nations is wider than it was a couple of decades ago; the same is true of the gap between rich and poor sectors in each Latin American country. The middle classes have almost disappeared, submerged in poverty. Thus we have what is called "neodualism": the population increasingly falls at the two ends of the economic and social spectrum. We speak of the 1980s as a "lost decade," which in some countries has actually been a longer period. But we should also note that in this period these countries have learned to develop clearer strategies for alleviating or resolving their problems.

Much has also changed in the international panorama. The fall of authoritarian socialism, which did not respect the basic rights of persons or consider the diversity of human aspirations, has led us from a bipolar world to a unipolar one in the political and military sphere; clearly the situation is more complex in the economic sphere. This has also led to a reaffirmation of the economic role of the market, although that role must be fulfilled within certain parameters which reflect vast social and human concerns. A technological revolution in the sphere of knowledge has radically transformed the process of fluctuating interest in the raw materials supplied by the poor countries; that change renders obsolete many of the categories by which we used to understand economic phenomena. The oppressive burden of external debt has distorted the economy of the poor countries, and the rigidity of the corresponding international organisms has acted as a straitjacket to limit each country's ability to meet the needs of the poorest people.

As a result new relationships have developed between North and South. These often increase the inequalities, which may grow to immeasurable proportions; the result is a growing threat to world peace, even if people think that economic and military power are able to control the situation for now.

Neoliberal ideology (one of whose slogans, with unintended irony, proclaims "the end of history") has its own way of reading the historical future of humanity; it dispossesses the poor nations of their past and disguises an economic and social process that is increasing the imbalance. In fact economic neoliberalism is already showing signs of decay that could change that picture in the future, but the current trend is clear.

On the other hand, the passage of time has given us a better understanding of the real situation of the poor and oppressed in Latin America. Early in the development of liberation theology we spoke of subjected peoples, exploited social classes, devalued races, and marginalized cultures. Then concern arose for the discrimination that women suffer: often a subtle attitude that became a habit, everyday life, a cultural tradition, but nonetheless harsh and senseless. Certainly these diverse concerns did not suddenly spring up with full-blown demands; they have appeared in recent years as a result of deepening solidarity with the world of the poor. Indeed the racial, cultural, and gender factors are increasingly important for a clearer understanding of the poor in Latin America. Because of this commitment we are gradually gaining awareness that in the last analysis — without ever forgetting its economic and social dimensions — poverty means death, unjust, early death.

Thus we affirm life as the primary human right and, from a Christian viewpoint, as a gift of God which must be defended. This affirmation began to mark our experience and reflection at the end of the 1970s (in Peru and Central America, for example) and has become the catalyst for many efforts and commitments. It has helped us to recover an evangelical perspective (so important to people like Las Casas in the sixteenth century) on the idolatrous nature of human profit as promoted by "savage capitalism," which tramples the dignity of human beings and turns them into the victims of a cruel and sacrilegious cult.

At the same time it is important to observe that poverty is not only a matter of not having. The poor are brimming with abilities and possibilities. The poor often possess a culture with its own values, from their race, their history, and their language; with energies like those shown in the struggle for life by women's organizations throughout the continent; with inventive and creative power that resists, against all odds, what today is being called the crisis of paradigms. This is a poor people who, although events have weakened — sometimes seriously weakened — their presence and energies, refuse to let their hope be mutilated or manipulated.

Open Questions

Many questions bubble up: How can people liberate themselves from the conditioning factors present on the international scene, which prevent the establishment of a just and human world? Who are the new social actors, who are the poor today? Can the countries of the South present and carry out their own projects, based on their tradition and on their needs? How can we assure access for the poor nations to scientific and technological knowledge, which today represents the dividing line between poverty and wealth? What conclusions should we draw from the discussion on dependency theory? What is the role of these peoples' historical memory in their struggle for justice? How should we understand poverty and better identify its causes? What role can the market economy play, within the limits defined here, in the establishment of a just society? What are the utopias and the mobilizing paths for those who want to overcome a situation of marginalization and abandonment? What is the relationship between liberation and development today?

Every question, once formulated, contains the shape of an answer. Total perplexity does not lead to questions; it does not have the energy to ask. But it is clear that the greatest task still lies ahead. There are important searches to undertake in Latin America; in this seminar we are trying to sound them out. They are crucial to the historical effectiveness of our defense of life and to the establishment of a just and human world. The only intelligent way to talk about social theories is to be aware that they lead to actions which affect the real, daily existence of human persons.

We have already pointed out how important these questions are for the evangelizing task and for theology. It is true that they come from the sphere of the social sciences but the social sciences are not ideologically neutral. The subjects they deal with are too delicate and complex to permit neutrality. It is important to be clear on this, so as not to be surreptitiously and uncritically taken in by ideas based on human and ethical positions.

An understanding of social and economic reality is key to an understanding of the faith, but we must also remember that each of these disciplines has its own sphere and methods. If we forget that, we will confuse theological reflection with the social sciences, and be relegated to ineffectiveness. We certainly are not promoting a strict separation between theology and economics or sociology; the important thing is to allow the instruments of analysis to do their best work without interference and keep the necessary distance to be alert to all the challenges of the situation.

There is a valid principle of distinguishing in order to unite. Let us approach the social interpretation of events with interest and respect; we have much to learn from it. Only in this way can we later establish the fruitful links that are needed for our understanding of and transformative action on real, challenging, and changing realities. Let us therefore make the distinctions, because the task of uniting our efforts is urgent.

— Translated by Margaret Wilde

PART THREE

Spirituality and Theology

As is known, an interest in spirituality has been present in the theology of liberation from the beginning. Discipleship of Jesus falls precisely in the realm of practice, upon which we are interested in reflecting in the light of the Word of the Lord. The experience of God is found in the heart of Christian spirituality, and that is, consequently, on the path taken by those who commit themselves, according to the messianic program of Jesus (see Luke 4:16–20), to proclaiming Good News to the poor and to liberation from all forms of oppression. The silence which marks the encounter with God nourishes all talk about God.

In this terrain, in that of a spirituality incarnate in the life of a people, a spirituality that doesn't disregard their most elemental necessities, the understanding of faith sinks its roots. At the same time, it achieves its full meaning in serving the task of evangelization. Theology fulfills its task in the heart of the community of disciples. But, at the same time, the community must be attentive to what occurs beyond the Church, in the world in which it lives, and in the paths necessary to understand the world with sympathy and discernment. The diversity in theology — within the framework of faith — is a result of the sensitivity of the different Christian communities to the contributions and challenges of human history in view of the Gospel witness.

– 7 –

John of the Cross
A Latin American View

Before trying to express the reason for my interest in a person like John of the Cross, it seems right to present, from the beginning, the difficulty — apparent or real — that such an interest raises for one who has had the experience as a citizen and as a Christian of a reality like that of Latin America. I come from a continent in which more than 60 percent of the population lives in a situation which experts call "poverty" or "extreme poverty" or destitution. This means that persons do not manage to satisfy their basic needs and, in the case of the destitute, lack the most elemental things. I come from a continent where in the past twenty years more than a hundred sisters, brothers, priests, and bishops have been assassinated and where hundreds of common people, catechists, and members of Christian communities have also been assassinated.

From Latin America

I come from a country in which about 60 percent (more than the average in Latin America) of the population finds itself in a situation of poverty (12 million people in a population of 22 million) and 25 percent (or 5 million people) live in extreme poverty. It is a country where 120 of every 1,000 children die before reaching five years of age; a country where two of every 1,000 people

From a talk delivered to the Congreso Internacional Sanjuanista in Avila, Spain, 1991, on the occasion of the fourth centenary of the birth of St. John of the Cross. Translation published in James B. Nickoloff, ed., *Gustavo Gutiérrez: Essential Writings* (Maryknoll, N.Y.: Orbis Books, 1996).

suffer from tuberculosis, a disease which has already been eliminated by medicine; a country where cholera has this year affected
300,000 people, of whom 3,000 have died. This disease is a disease of the poor because it is caused by a very fragile virus which
dies at a temperature of 140 degrees. But the poor suffer from it
because they lack the economic means to boil water or to prepare
food in sanitary conditions. I come from a country in which approximately 25,000 people have died as victims of different kinds
of violence and where eight priests and religious have been assassinated, three of them in recent weeks. They all worked in poor
regions of my country.

I am one of those Christians who in Latin America believe that
poverty is contrary to the will of God. We believe that solidarity with the poor person and the fight for justice are unavoidable
Christian demands. For this reason I am one of those Christians
who are frequently asked about our fidelity to the Church and
about our orthodoxy or heterodoxy. We are asked — with suspi-
cion — where our place is in this Church in which we were born,
with which we receive communion, and from which we try to
understand the situation of our continent.

Given these realities and these difficulties, of what interest
could the saint of the "Ascent of Mount Carmel" be to us? Do not
the dark nights, the purifications, the betrothals with God seem
very far from daily life? This saint for whom themes such as social justice seem foreign, who never commented on nor even cited
Luke 4:16 or Matthew 25:31 — of what interest can he be for us?
These are important texts in the lived experience of Christians in
Latin America and in my own reflections. How can we be drawn
to this great Christian whom we may admire but who seems far
from our concerns?

How to Say That God Loves Us?

It would be tempting and fun to play what-might-have-been.
For example, we might imagine John of the Cross in Mexico
(where he was supposed to go, sent into a kind of exile) living his
faith on a continent which in previous decades had lost perhaps 80

percent of its population. But circumstances determined that John of the Cross would go to what he delightfully called the "Minor Indies," to an encounter with the Father. It would be tempting also, and a bit more serious, to recall his familiarity with poverty as a religious and the persecution he suffered due to his concern for reform. Perhaps along this path we could find a bridge which links us to him. We could also poke through his writings and find texts such as the one in which he condemns the satisfied who are repulsed by the poor — which, says the saint, is contrary to the will of God.

But I honestly do not believe that the main reason John of the Cross is of interest to the present reality of Latin America is to be found in such approaches. I think that we need to look for it elsewhere, not because what I have said is not important but because it is not exactly for these reasons that his witness and work are relevant for us.

There are persons who are universal due to the extent of their knowledge, their direct influence on their times, or the diversity and number of their disciples. Erasmus might be an example of this type of universality in the sixteenth century. But there are also those who are universal because of the intensity of their lives and their thought. More than traversing the world with their ideas, they go to the very center of it and thus find themselves equidistant from everything that happens on the surface. John of the Cross is one of them, universal because of his singularity — of a concrete universality, Hegel would say. If this is the case, if John of the Cross is a universal man for these reasons, he would not be alien to what is happening in Latin America. And he is not.

On our continent we pose for ourselves a lacerating question: How to say to the poor person, to the oppressed person, to the insignificant person, God loves you? Indeed, the daily life of the poor seems to be the result of the denial of love. The absence of love is, in the final analysis of faith, the cause of social injustice. The question of how to tell the poor person "God loves you" is much greater than our capacity to answer it. Its breadth, to use a phrase very dear to John of the Cross, makes our answers very small. But the question is there, unavoidable, demanding, challenging. Is not the work of John of the Cross a titanic effort to tell us that God loves us? Is our interest (as Latin Americans) in his witness and work not to be found right there, in the very heart of Christian revelation? Was John of the Cross not someone who made an immense effort to tell us that when everything is over, our "care," our concern about how to tell the poor person that God is Love, will remain "forgotten among white lilies"?

An Experience of Faith

I will try to point out several features of his writings which question us and help us and thus are read by us. However, before entering into these matters I want to say that we Christians in Latin America are convinced that what is at stake in our people's efforts to achieve an all-encompassing and complex, multifaceted liberation is our way of being Christians, our very faith, our hope, and our love. We have always had the conviction that this commitment is not to be limited to the field of social justice, though this is of primary importance, but that we do not see a different way of being followers of the Lord, of being disciples of Jesus. Our being Christian is at stake: here John of the Cross reappears, and powerfully, because for him too what is at stake is a way of being Christian. In Latin America we try to live what we call — using a formula which today has become universal — the option for the poor, the preferential option for the poor person, as a spiritual experience, that is, as an experience of the Lord. This is very clear in the Christian communities throughout the continent. In this spiritual experience, how — in what way and for what reasons — does the witness of John of the Cross become relevant and important for us? I will present five points, among others, in an attempt to answer this question.

Gratuitousness

Something profoundly biblical appears in his witness and work: the gratuitousness of God's love. Now there is nothing more demanding than gratuitousness. Duty has a ceiling, it goes up to a certain point and is satisfied when an obligation is fulfilled. This is not the case with the gratuitousness of love because love has no border. When Paul tells Philemon (in a letter widely overlooked by Christians) "I know that you will do more than I ask you," it is a suggestion completely open to permanent creativity. There is nothing which is more demanding than gratuitous love. John of the Cross has reminded us that to be a believer is to think that God is enough. The night of the senses and the spiritual night ought to strip us, and finally liberate us, from idolatries. In the Bible idolatry is a danger to every believer. Idolatry means trusting in something or someone other than God, giving our lives over to what we have made with our own hands. We frequently offer victims to such an idol, which is why the prophets link idolatry and murder so often.

St. John of the Cross helps us to discover a faith which does not rest on idols, on mediation. This is why the biblical figure Job is so important to him. It is not strange that he would call Job a prophet. He is right; Job was a prophet. A study of the vocabulary of the Book of Job places him closer to the prophetic books than to the wisdom books....

We in Latin America are also convinced — and John of the Cross helps us to understand this — that in the liberation process we are capable of creating our own idols for ourselves. For example, the idol of justice: it might seem strange to say this but justice can become an idol if it is not placed in the context of gratuity, if there is no real friendship with the poor person nor daily commitment with him or her. Gratuity is the framework for justice and gives it meaning in history. Social justice, no matter how important it is — and it is — can also be an idol, and we have to purify ourselves of this to affirm very clearly that only God suffices and to give justice itself the fullness of its meaning.

In the same way the poor person to whom we wish to commit ourselves and with whom we wish to live in solidarity can become an idol. An example of this is the idealization of the poor person by some in Latin America as if they had to demonstrate to themselves and to others that every poor person is good, generous, religious, and for that reason we have to be committed to him or her.... I would also like to make clear — because I say this with great conviction — that another idol can be our own theology, the theology we are trying to formulate in Latin America beginning with the reality of suffering and of hope found in our people.... Once again, with the scalpel of his experience and poetry, John of the Cross eliminates what is infected, what blurs our vision of God. Furthermore, in one of his texts, John of the Cross reminds us of a fundamental biblical datum: our love for God grows to the degree that our love of neighbor grows. And vice versa.

To finish this point, which I consider the most important, I would like to read a very brief verse by a Spanish priest assassinated in Bolivia, Luis Espinal: "Lord of the night and of the void, we yearned to know how to sink softly into your impalpable lap confidently, with the security of children." This is what we mean by the liberation process. I have always thought this.

The Journey

This is a particularly expressive and telling theme in John of the Cross. It takes up a fertile biblical image. A journey presupposes time and history, and this time and this history have a very peculiar meaning in John of the Cross, so much so that they can pass unseen.... In his work there is movement, displacement, advance, yet there he is, in the same place. There is great mobility and a very profound sense of history or of time and simultaneously a fixation on God.... In Deuteronomy we have an explanation for an apparently banal question which Christians sometimes do not ask themselves but which was important to the Jews: why did the Jewish people take forty years to cross the desert from Egypt to Palestine? Even crawling on your knees it would not take forty years....

In Deuteronomy the explanation has to do with a twofold knowledge: so that the people can come to know God and God (anthropomorphically speaking) can come to know the people. This explains the long crossing. And this, it seems to me, is what we also find in John of the Cross. On the journey there is a twofold knowing. As he says, we leave in order to arrive; we don't leave in order to journey, but we journey in order to arrive. We leave one place in order to get to another. This knowledge comes in a dialogue with God.

We in Latin America are seeking to understand the liberation process as a journey not only to social freedom (which is very important) but equally and above all toward full friendship with God and among ourselves. This is, once again, what we understand by the formula "preferential option for the poor." This is the journey and we believe that it implies time.... In the final analysis, the option for the poor is a theocentric option, a life centered on God — just as John of the Cross desired.

Freedom

The famous phrase "There is no way through here" does not denote the easiest stretch of the ascent but the most difficult. Up to this point it was possible to follow a marked path; from this point one must continue creatively and with steadiness. John of the Cross lived out this freedom when he chose to be a discalced Carmelite, when he refused to give in to pressures to renounce that condition, when he escaped from prison. We can call it freedom, but there is another way to name this attitude: stubbornness. John was pigheaded — like all saints (which does not mean that all hard-headed people are saints). It is a spiritual attitude: "Where the Spirit is there is freedom," according to the famous phrase of St. Paul.

In Latin America we understand freedom as the goal of liberation; liberation is not our end but a process, the journey and not the point of arrival. We have also experienced during this time that this journey toward freedom is not something marked out beforehand.... "Free to love" is a formula we frequently use to speak of our way of understanding what it means to be a Christian. ... This is the freedom which matters to us and that is why John of the Cross, like every spiritual person, is a free man and thus is often so dangerous. That is how many of his contemporaries saw him. That is how many Christians in Latin America are seen.

Joy

St. John of the Cross spoke of joy. It is very present in the songs, in the Spiritual Canticle, where the image of the love of a human couple — a profound experience of joy — allows him to speak of the joy of the encounter with the Lord. At the same time this is a joy lived out in the midst of difficulty, ascending the slope of a mountain in the midst of suffering. I do not know (though there are outstanding scholars here who could comment on this with a competence that I do not have), but I think that the experience of poverty of John of Yepes, the fact of having been poor, must have marked him with a profound feeling of pain. Indeed, the experience of the poor person is that of being insignificant and marginal. To have seen his mother begging, to have begged for alms himself, are very profound experiences. Our contact today with the poor makes us see that their lives remain marked not by sadness but by a profound pain. And this is why they appreciate more than others the reason for being happy. Perhaps his experience of prison, in which he even feared losing his life, is part of this suffering. His joy therefore is, to put it in Christian terms, paschal, an overcoming of suffering, a passage to joy. I would say that at present in Latin America there is no way to be close to the poor without entering into communion with their pain and with their reason for joy. As Christians we feel loved by God, the fundamental reason for our joy.

But as I said a moment ago, suffering does not necessarily signify sadness....Sadness is the turning in on oneself which is located on the border of bitterness; suffering, on the contrary, can create in us a space of solitude, a space for gaining personal depth. Solitude is another important theme in John of the Cross, solitude as the condition of an authentic communion. After all, Jesus' cry "My God, why have you abandoned me?" was shouted forth on the eve of the greatest communion in history, that of the resurrection, that of the life that conquers death. Solitude is, then, a requirement for communion.

Language

John of the Cross affirms that he is trying to approach the themes mentioned here by beginning with experience, science, and equally—as he nicely puts it—by "cuddling up with Scripture." The result is poetry in verse or in prose. And poetry is doubtless the greatest human gift a person can receive. How can we speak of love without poetry? Love is the thing that has always given rise to poetry. From this continent marked by unjust and premature death, we also think that experience is the necessary condition to be able to speak about God and to say to the poor person: God loves you. Experience of the mystery of God.

I have always admired those philosophers and theologians who speak about what God thinks and wants as if they had breakfast with God every day. John of the Cross reminds us, however, that this is impossible, that we can speak of God and the love of God only with great respect, aware of what his master Thomas Aquinas said: "What we don't know about God is much greater than what we know." Without being about to understand things well but convinced that he must love, the Peruvian poet and a dear friend Gonzalo Rose said, "Why should I have loved the rose and justice? Yet this is what we are called to do in Latin America: to love justice and beauty. God is the source of both. Our language about God, that is, our theology, must take both of these aspects into account."

I began by saying that I come from a continent marked by death, but I also want to say that I come from a continent in which a people is undergoing an exceedingly profound experience of life. This is expressed when people organize so that their most elementary rights will be respected; it is also expressed in their rich religious life. From this experience the poor of our continent — without using the word "mystical" — express a profound sense of God. This lived experience does not contradict their poverty or their suffering. And I want to tell you that I come from a continent (this may sound excessively optimistic) where there is great holiness and generous and anonymous self-giving. There are many people who live in extremely difficult areas, who risk their physical life between the two kinds of gunfire that today kill people in my country — hunger and cruel, brutal terrorism.

Just a year ago today they killed Sister of the Good Shepherd María Agustina Rivas, called "Aguchita," a seventy-year-old woman. A little before going to work in the place where she was assassinated, which was jokingly called "Florida," this woman wrote a letter in which she said, "I want to go work with the poor of Florida because I do not want to present myself to the Lord with empty hands." If she presented herself with full hands, it is because she humbly believed that they were empty.

Finally, I would like to say that there is something which is being lived out today with great intensity in Latin America: the value of life. Ignacio Ellacuría often said, "Here in El Salvador life is worthless." He was wrong; his own example gives the lie to his affirmation. The life of Salvadorans had to be worth a lot to him to make him and his companions remain in El Salvador. There were people of great intellectual gifts and at the same time committed to that country to the point of risking their lives. The lives of Salvadorans had to be worth a lot in order for them to do this.

We are more and more convinced that death is not the last word of history; life is. That is why Christian celebrations always mock death: "Death, where is your victory?" Every feast is an Easter. Perhaps this is why in the Hispanic tradition we call all the feasts "Easter" (*pascua*). We are the only people in the world who say "Happy Easter" (*"Felices pascuas"*) at Christmas — and at Epiphany. (Pentecost used to be an "Easter" too.) Every Christian feast is an Easter, a Passover, because we celebrate the defeat of death.

Let me conclude in what is perhaps not an academic way. I would like to ask you to keep in your prayers and your thoughts this people which resists accepting early and unjust death. We Christians must say, with that great Spaniard Bartolomé de Las Casas, "of the smallest and most forgotten God has a very fresh and living memory." This fresh and living memory permits them to keep their hopes high. I ask you to keep in mind those of my continent who can say with that great Peruvian poet César Vallejo, "I have nothing but death with which to express my life." This is the situation of many Christians, and this is why John of the Cross — he of the nights, he of the solitude, he of the journey, he of the encounter with God — is not foreign to us.

— Translated by James B. Nickoloff

– 8 –

Friends of God, Friends of the Poor

We recently celebrated the thirtieth anniversary of the closing of the Second Vatican Council. On that occasion Paul VI gave a profound and important address, explaining the meaning of the Council.

He said: "The ancient story of the Samaritan has been the spiritual beacon of the Council. An immense sympathy has penetrated it throughout. The discovery of human needs...has absorbed the attention of our synod." Indeed that was the attitude of the Council toward the people of our world to whom the Gospel is proclaimed. Paul VI anticipated subsequent misinterpretations of the Council, emphasizing that its inspiration was profoundly religious: "in the face of every man, especially when his tears and sorrows make it transparent, we can and must recognize the face of Christ, the Son of Man" (see Matt. 25:40). Thus, he added, "our humanism becomes Christianity, our Christianity becomes theocentric, so that we can also affirm: in order to know God we must know man."[1] In this way the Council opened new avenues for hope.

The words of Paul VI also describe the recent General Congregations of the Company of Jesus, which have rightly sought to follow the path laid out by Vatican II. The Thirty-Fourth General Congregation (hereafter CG 34), which took place last year, forcefully and wisely drew on the two preceding ones, and also

---

Published in *Cuadernos de Espiritualidad* 73 (January–March 1996): 47–56.

1. *Valor religioso del Concilio* (December 7, 1965).

on Ignatian tradition. These assemblies have sought to find ways of serving the Lord, which necessarily leads them to commitment with the beloved of the Lord: the poor. Their concern for justice is essentially theocentric, but they know that in order to know God it is also necessary to know the human being.

The purpose of these pages is to analyze the four decrees of CG 34 which follow the Introduction, and which are gathered under the title: "Our Mission." They are dense texts, from which we can only emphasize a few central points, perhaps in order to see the scope of others more clearly.

Discerning the Signs of the Times

The unique and prophetic figure of John XXIII set the course for the Council. He said that if today we want to say "thy kingdom come," we must be attentive to history, "obeying Jesus' instructions to discern the signs of the times" (Matt. 16:4).[2] This idea was dear to Pope John; he repeated it shortly before his death and linked it to one of his key ideas: the Church's need "to see far off."[3] The Council embraced this insight of John XXIII and used it to approach human history in order to hear the Word of God (see *Gaudium et Spes,* 4).

CG 34 is a great and fruitful attempt to discern the signs of our times as a community. Indeed it says that the reading of those signs "is the effort to discern the presence and activity of God in the real events of contemporary history, in order to decide what we must do as servants of the Word" (d. 16, 7).[4] This attitude recalls a great Ignatian theme, drawn from the first great point of the Spiritual Exercises: the discernment of spirits. What is at stake is how to serve the Word, how to proclaim the Gospel. This is the mission of the Church, and therefore of all who belong to it.

---

2. He went on to say that in this way we can perceive "in the midst of dark shadows more than a few signs that seem to promise better times for the Church and for humanity" (in the constitution convoking the Council, *Humanae salutis,* December 25, 1961).

3. See *Diary of a Soul.*

4. See also CG 32, d. 4,10.

The four decrees mentioned above are about that mission and its demands today.

We need to understand that mission in its broadest and deepest sense; that is another of the great contributions of Vatican II. One of the best theological works of the Council — the first five numbers of the decree on missionary activity, *Ad Gentes* — traces the roots of the Church's mission to the trinitarian missions of the Son and the Holy Spirit. The Ignatian mystique, which is above all a trinitarian mystique (see the *Spiritual Diary*), would find itself in full agreement with that approach.

The concept of mission offered in *Ad Gentes* goes beyond the proclamation of the Gospel to non-Christians; it defines the Church itself as "missionary by nature" (AG 2). This task is realized in earthly time; therefore its specific paths vary according to the challenges of each age. The Church has a single mission, the "prophetic proclamation of the Gospel," but it is carried out through diverse ministries (CG 34, d. 2,5–6). We must learn which ones the Lord is calling us to perform "at the crossroads of cultural conflicts, social and economic struggles, religious renewal and new opportunities." We urgently need to read it with eyes of faith, to discern in those events the paths we must take "to carry the Good News to the people of the whole world" (d. 2,2).

That discernment was the goal of the General Congregation. It is not a purely intellectual operation; it implies the participants' determination to place themselves at the service of the faith "in solidarity with the poor according to our Ignatian charism" (d. 2,8). One feature of that charism is commitment, and persistence, in that which gives meaning to "the present pilgrimage" toward the Father.[5] One anecdote from the life of Ignatius will illustrate what we have just said, and show how seriously "the pilgrim," as he used to call himself (see his autobiography), took his earthly voyage.

Fr. Ribadeneira relates that one time (he even gives the date) Ignatius asked Diego Láinez: "What would you do if the Lord God

5. Letter from Ignatius of Loyola to Antonio Enríquez (154) in *Obras de Ignacio de Loyola* (Madrid, 1991), 993.

asked you: if you wish to die, I will release you from the prison of this body and give you eternal glory, but if you wish to go on living, I give you no assurance about what will happen to you; you will be left to your fate. . . . How would you reply?" In his reply the teacher Láinez chose the first alternative. Ignatius then replied: "Well, I certainly would not do so; if I believed that by remaining in this life I could do some special service to our Lord, I would beg him to leave me here until I had done that service; and I would place my eyes on him and not on me, without regard for my danger or security."[6]

I hope the old-fashioned style in which the story is told will not keep us from seeing the audacity of Ignatius's position. Clearly it is not that he doesn't want to enjoy soon what St. Paul called the "face to face" with God; that is what gave meaning to his life, as Ignatius repeated (quoted a few lines after this story). The point that the anecdote expresses so simply is his deep love for a God who acts in history and his aspiration to go on collaborating with that task. The discernment of the signs of the times must be animated by a conviction of service, by a militant spirit. Otherwise it is only self-serving knowledge, which does not lead to commitment to those whom the Lord loves and whom he wants to reach with his word. Nothing could be further from the Ignatian spirit.

The Integrating Principle

The discernment of which we speak leads to a discussion of what CG 34 calls "the integrating principle of our mission" (d. 2,7), that is, the factor which gives an organic character to "all our ministries" (d. 2,14). That makes this a key point. In a way it is dictated by the historical reality in which the participants sought to understand the Lord's call. CG 34 presents this integrating principle as "the inseparable link between faith and promotion of the justice of the kingdom" (d. 2,14). Thus it picks up the central insight of the Thirty-Second General Congregation (1974–75),

---

6. *Vida de San Ignacio de Loyola* (Madrid, 1951), 404–5.

which left a fruitful mark on the life of the Company of Jesus.[7] "The promotion of justice" is seen by the order "as an integrating part of its mission," in response to the summons of Vatican II (d. 2,1).

Faith and justice thus stand at the poles of a rich tension, sometimes accompanied by misunderstandings and simplistic interpretations (see d. 2,3). The newness of this formulation (it is in fact an old biblical idea) made such difficulties inevitable. CG 34 is fully aware of them, and chooses its words prudently to avoid later misunderstandings; but the text also broadens its vision and acquires a maturity which does not diminish the firmness of its positions on the issue. What is important is that this tension helps us to see the demands of the Gospel today.

Then new dimensions are added to the concern for justice. Let us emphasize two that are particularly important to us. First, human rights, which are so battered in Peru in our day: the document sees these as the rights of persons and also of peoples (see d. 3,6). The text also places value on ecological balance and the equitable use of worldly resources as "important elements of justice" in today's world, basing this perspective on "protection of the integrity of creation" (d. 3,9). These are clearly some of the aspects, among others, which urgently challenge the Church in its evangelizing task. We are therefore called to carry out in specific ways what Pius XI and his successors have called "the noble struggle for justice." That task is still very important.

In this regard CG 34 proposes "to create communities of solidarity in the search for justice" (d. 3,19) and affirms "full human liberation, for the poor and for all of us" (d. 3,10) as the basis of its development. This is an interesting idea, but many things must

---

7. "The mission of the Company of Jesus today is the service of the faith, in which the promotion of justice is an absolute requirement" (CG 32, d. 4,2). Later the same Congregation adds, therefore: "evangelization is a proclamation of the faith which acts in the love of humanity (Gal. 5:5; Eph. 4:15) and cannot be truly carried out without the promotion of justice" (d. 4,28). CG 32 acknowledges its debt to the synods "Justice in the World" and "Evangelization of the Contemporary World" (see d. 4,32). But we must not forget the "Letter from the Provincials of the Company of Jesus in Latin America" (May 1968), which in clear language addressed the problems of poverty and injustice.

still be clarified if we want it to be more than wishful thinking. Above all they must be put in practice; the criterion of "greater fruit" (in the constitutions) will judge their value and scope in the complex reality that we are living in this country (see d. 3,22).

In the time since CG 32, commitment to those who suffer injustice leads us to see that the "mission of service to the faith and promotion of justice must be broadened" (d. 2,20). This is one of the most significant contributions of CG 34. The Congregation seeks to broaden "the integrating principle" of faith-justice by incorporating "the inculturated proclamation of the Gospel and dialogue with other religious traditions" (d. 2,15).[8] This is a perceptive note: cultures and religions play a relevant part in the promotion of justice. This is a decisive reason to bring the Gospel into dialogue with them (see d. 2,17).[9]

It is truly a question of dialogue. Two voices, and also two silences, are needed if people are to listen to each other. "To incarnate the Word of God in the diversity of human experience" (d. 4,3) means being attentive to the cultures they express and appreciating their values. It also implies "not being bound to any [culture] in particular" (d. 4,2). This last is hard to put in practice in a Church so deeply rooted in Western culture. It is a passionate and ongoing task; what is at stake today is what Karl Rahner called "the true universality" of the Church, which he sees as beginning with Vatican II.[10]

In this context the document is sensitive to an issue full of repercussions in a country like ours: "among the indigenous peoples there has been a growing awareness of their cultures, which should be supported with the liberating power of the Gospel" (d. 4,5.4). That is also true in other countries, but the Peruvian Church should take note of it in carrying out a respectful evangelization within our national borders.

The presence of the Church — and the Company — in dif-

---

8. The episcopal conference at Santo Domingo (1992) had already made the inculturation of the Gospel one of its central themes.
9. One text beautifully presents the relationships among evangelization, justice, cultures, and religions (see d. 2,19).
10. *Concern for the Church* (New York: Crossroad, 1981), 77–78.

ferent areas of humanity leads to another important theme: inter-religious dialogue. Here too Vatican II opened the way; that dialogue has also been a constant concern of John Paul II. The Church must enrich itself with the religious experience of all humanity and present with conviction, but with humility, the Gospel of Jesus Christ. This means acknowledging that "the Word of God has been communicated to those religions and that the salvific presence of the Holy Spirit is in them" (d. 5,6). That conviction does not diminish our evangelical witness, but helps us find the appropriate forms and ways for carrying it out.

The text often notes the relationship of both culture and religion to the promotion of justice in the context of authentic service to the faith. There is much to learn from this will to unification, which does not forget the difference among the various aspects involved, but which also keeps in mind both the common source and the one final destiny of those human dimensions.

Solidarity with the Poor

The spiritual discernment of which we speak leads us to take a position on something greater: world poverty. By deepening and broadening the link between faith and justice, we can more adequately and fruitfully grasp the incisive challenge of poverty. We know this from experience, and the text makes it clear from the beginning: "our service, especially to the poor, has deepened our life of faith" (d. 2,1).

And it has given us new eyes for seeing. That is true of one famous letter from Ignatius to the Jesuit community at Padua, which the document quotes at length. CG 34 calls it "a prophetic text for our time," because it reads "with new eyes" (d. 2,8). "The eye of our intention," as Ignatius says in the preamble, sharpens our vision and allows us to discover in this old, often-read text, implications which we never suspected before but which fit the demands of our age, through which the Lord's will is expressed.

The letter reminds us that Christ was sent "primarily" for the poor, that "he preferred them to the rich," and that he chose them as his closest collaborators and advisors. Thus, Ignatius concludes, "friendship with the poor makes us friends of the eternal King."[11] The document comments rightly: "Thus to be friends of the Lord means to be friends of the poor" (d. 2,9). The Introduction to CG 34 described the members of the Company as "friends in the Lord" (d. 1,10 and d. 2,1), and here the idea is explained: "we are a community in solidarity with the poor precisely because of Christ's preferential love for them" (d. 2,9).[12] That solidarity must keep in mind "this our world of such diversity" of culture (d. 3,18). Indeed the poor are not only those who lack economic resources; they also belong to a culture, a religion, a gender. The complexity of this situation makes it a many-sided challenge.

Here the document speaks of real (sometimes called material) poverty, which has human and historical causes and at whose roots is the brokenness of friendship with God: that is, sin. The language is precise: "the sin of the world, which Christ came to heal, reaches its culmination in our time in social structures which exclude the poor (the immense majority of the world population) from participation in the benefits of creation" (d. 2,9). The structural causes of poverty have been denounced by the Church — not without resistance and hostility — in recent decades (see the Latin American episcopal conferences and, with special insistence, the magisterium of John Paul II).[13]

Poverty and its causes are opposed to the will to life and fellowship with God that are inscribed in God's creation. On this point the document quotes a fitting text of Fr. Kolvenbach: "God has always been the God of the poor because the poor are visible proof of a failure in the work of creation" (d. 2,9). There is no room

---

11. Letter to the fathers and brothers of Padua (August 7, 1547). Written by J. A. Polanco under the guidance of Ignatius. Not only one passage, but the whole letter centers on the theme of poverty and the poor and on the implications of that theme for the Company of Jesus.

12. Later: "Solidarity with the poor which cannot only be a concern for some Jesuits; it must characterize our life and our ministries" (d. 9,16). See also the important text of d. 26,14.

13. A similar approach is found in CG 32, d. 4,32 and in CG 33, n. 83. CG 34 points out that "unrestrained capitalism" leads to the exclusion of the poor mentioned above.

for the idealization of poverty; as Medellín[14] and Latin American theology have made very clear, poverty is an evil. This is an incontrovertible truth, though it is not as widely recognized as one might wish.

From this viewpoint we can understand without equivocation some other relevant references to poverty in CG 34 and in a variety of other texts from Christian sources. For example, there is the need to embrace poverty as a condition of credibility for the evangelizing task (see d. 9,6), or the choice of "poverty with the poor Christ" as a distinctive mark of all disciples and an expression of their spiritual poverty (d. 1,5). This is voluntary poverty for the love of God and the poor, but it does not in any way mean that believers should cease to judge and reject the poverty that so many people are suffering in today's world.

The decrees of CG end with some concrete recommendations. These are guidelines for putting in practice the options taken by the assembly. They require the decisive "conversion of the heart" alluded to by Fr. Kolvenbach in his closing homily to the Congregation (CG 34, p. 495), without which the full value of the texts is diminished. These reflections and norms suggest a way, set a direction, create consensus; but what Ignatius of Loyola said in the Proemio to the constitutions of the Company is true of CG 34: "more than any outward constitution, the inward law of charity and love that the Holy Spirit writes and stamps on the heart will help" (134). The way opened by the Spirit within us will help us to find our way — even without pathmarks to follow — to the Father and to our brothers and sisters.

That is the meaning of Christian freedom under the action of the Spirit, freedom to love (Gal. 5:1 and 13) as St. Paul says in words that appropriately describe Ignatian spirituality. This indeed is love, and as Ignatius says at the beginning of "Contemplation Reaching Toward Love," "love must be placed more in works than in words" (*Spiritual Exercises,* n. 230). This is where we find friendship with the poor and friendship with the Lord in a world that denies them in so many ways.

---

14. "Poverty" 4.

This is demanding and inspiring guidance, which goes against inertia and calls for deep changes,[15] for all those who embrace the decrees of the Thirty-Fourth General Congregation and take on an evangelizing task in our time. It is open to the future, and it is in our hands as long as we lovingly, respectfully place our hands in God's.

— Translated by Margaret Wilde

---

15. Remembering the turning point of CG 32, Father Arrupe referred to solidarity with the poor as "a change of mentality…transforming our way of being in order to transform our way of acting" (*L'espérance ne trompe pas* [Paris: Le Centurion, 1981], 112).

– 9 –

From Exclusion to Discipleship

While I do not intend to offer this as a general definition of what we mean by mysticism, it is clear that it has something to do with an experience of God in a key of love, peace, and joy. In contrast, "oppression" refers to a situation of poverty, injustice, and exclusion, with its resultant suffering and, in many cases, rejection and rebellion. Are these then incompatible human experiences?

On this abstract conceptual level, perhaps the question requires the answer "yes." On the other hand, as a matter of fact those who find themselves in these situations are human beings, with all the personal dimensions this implies; they also belong to peoples with a history, culture, and vision of the universe. Only in this real context can we fruitfully explore this subject. In doing so we meet people in whom poverty and dispossession mark their faith in God, and this in its turn leaves a mark on the condition of oppression and discrimination.[1]

There is certainly a close relationship between mysticism and politics, which has been the subject of many studies. Without contemplation, prayer, thanksgiving to God there is no Christian life, any more than there is without commitment, solidarity, and love of neighbor. The point I am making now is certainly connected with this relationship, but it is not identical with it. Our

Published in Christian Duquoc and Gustavo Gutiérrez, eds., *Mysticism and the Institutional Church*, Concilium (1994/4).

1. In Latin America for many years now we have talked about a "people that is oppressed and Christian." In an Asian context Aloysius Pieris refers to the way "*Poverty* and *Religiosity* seem to coalesce"; see "Towards an Asian Theology of Liberation," *The Month* 1340 (May 1979): 148 (italics in original).

question is rather: can we talk of a mystical dimension in the faith life of a person who suffers exclusion and injustice and eventually embarks on a path of liberation from these conditions?

An attempt to answer this question presupposes a move from the realm of the individual to a position within sociocultural contexts and a historical perspective and to viewpoints from different geographical points on the planet. Above all, however, it requires us to be sensitive to one of the facts most pregnant with consequences for present-day Christianity: the Christian faith has not just begun to spring up, but has also grown and matured in non-Western peoples who have been poor and oppressed for centuries.

Today in the Church certain conflicts of interpretation about the times we live in and the challenges they present to us frequently provoke tension, difficulties, and misunderstandings that prevent us from seeing that something much more important than these differences of opinion — even on issues that are obviously important and even urgent — is taking place among us. In a famous article, a sort of balance-sheet of Vatican II, Karl Rahner said that the Council's main significance was that it marked the beginning of a third stage in the life of the Church, a period in which it could begin to be genuinely universal.[2]

The vigorous existence of local churches in places geographically and culturally far removed from Europe, the force of their voices, containing accents of pain and hope, the contribution of their theological reflection, and the new challenges this brings represent the most important event for the Christian faith in these final years of the second millennium of its history.[3]

This is the context in which we must discuss the subject of mysticism and oppression. The presence of those who are different from Western culture is now established, of course, but

2. See *Concern for the Church* (New York: Crossroad, 1981). From a theological standpoint, Rahner says, there are three main periods in the history of the Church: the period from Jesus to Paul, connected to the Jewish world; the time between Paul and Vatican II, linked to the Western world; and the third period, beginning with Vatican II.

3. This is why J. B. Metz uses the term "polycentric Church," replacing the monocentric Church, confined to the West. See "Theology in the Modern Age, and before Its End," *Concilium* 171 (January 1984): 13–17.

it is not always recognized; it will lead us to reexamine central texts of the Christian revelation which can throw light on the process under way and finally indicate the pattern of spirituality represented by the preferential option for the poor.

Assimilation and Otherness

The Europeans who came to the American continent in the sixteenth century (and from their point of view "discovered" it) were spontaneously and absolutely convinced of their human and cultural superiority to the inhabitants of these lands.[4] The peoples whom they began to call "Indians" had, in their eyes, no rights that could call in question the privileges in which they gloried as discoverers and conquerors. The fate of these peoples was to hand over all they possessed to the newcomers and finally to labor for them.

The majority of missionaries took the same view. As regards the Gospel, the Indians — lacking religious values — were simply *tabula rasa* (Columbus used the phrase in his diary), a blank page on which everything was still to be written. Some even thought this could be done by force and wars; others, to varying degrees, called for more human treatment, but the basic acceptance of the asymmetry between Europeans and the Indian population was the same.

In this perspective, the best fate that could befall the inhabitants of these lands was to be absorbed by the superior culture and religion. This policy of assimilation not only did not prevent prior destruction, it presupposed it and moreover presented itself as a form of destruction. This attitude, assimilationist and colonialist, has not died. The economic and political preponderance of the North Atlantic countries has kept it alive; even more, the power and ubiquitousness of the communications media have made this

---

4. The same thing happened, *mutatis mutandis,* in the contacts with African and Asian countries. I shall refer mainly to Latin America in this article because I know this situation better, but I have no doubt that the attitudes in question are not limited to this continent.

attitude an everyday reality, and to a great extent one generally accepted.

This mentality is also expressed in the Christian world. It would seem that many people believe there is no other way of being a believer in Jesus Christ than through the Western mental categories and lifestyle that trace their roots back to a Greco-Latin past. This is something that the Christian churches to this day have been unable to overcome. The result is a series of misunderstandings and unresolved problems that weigh heavily on the development of the ecclesial communities present in a world that is distant from or alien to that of the North Atlantic.[5]

However, as early as the sixteenth century itself a different attitude from the one we have just described was already present. A handful of missionaries reacted vigorously against the ill treatment of the Indians, and gradually some of them — notably Bartolomé de Las Casas — began to insist on respect for the culture and customs of the Indian nations. It was not easy for all of them to shake off the conviction of belonging to the highest level of civilization, and it could be said that in a sense they did not succeed in this completely and in all areas. But they journeyed firmly in this direction.

Las Casas believed that if we want to understand what is happening we have to adopt the point of view of the inhabitants of the Indies. "If we were Indians," the Dominican bishop said, "things would take on a different color for us." The discovery of otherness — a costly, but clear-sighted process — marks not only his pastoral action and theological method, but also his spirituality as a Christian. His enormous and bold attempt to understand from within, and to make his compatriots understand, the human sacrifices and the cannibalism practiced among the Aztecs — which scandalized the Europeans — is an example of how far he was able to go in this attempt.[6]

Recognizing otherness is still an unfinished task. This was one

---

5. We shall see what happens in this regard during the forthcoming (April–May 1994) synod of the Catholic bishops of Africa.

6. G. Gutiérrez, *Las Casas: In Search of the Poor of Jesus Christ* (Maryknoll, N.Y.: Orbis Books, 1993).

of the earliest intuitions of liberation theology.[7] The perspective of the "underside of history" is an obligation still in full force. The perception of the otherness of the poor and oppressed (in social, racial, cultural and gender terms) enables us to understand how they can enjoy a keen sense of God, which does not disdain celebration and joy, in the midst of a situation of expropriation and a struggle for justice. By unknown paths the experience of oppression has turned out to be fruitful ground for the mystical dimension of Christian life.

What seems contradictory or, at best, suspect, to a modern mentality becomes real and full of promise in a different socio-cultural context. And let no one think that I am talking about the practice of prayer as a protection against daily sufferings or religious observance as a shock absorber to deaden the reaction of rejection provoked by exploitation and contempt. Such situations exist, of course, and not just as exceptions, but they do not account for or explain the whole situation. There are many cases in which the mystical and spiritual perspective is, on the contrary, the best antidote to the use of Christianity as a search for a refuge or a justification of the status quo, and one of the main factors in generating and developing human and Christian solidarity.

Moreover, this complex experience provides criteria for discernment with results that seem simple, but are nonetheless unexpected. For example, I can never forget the distinction I heard made by a woman belonging to a Christian base community: a Christian can live joy in a situation of suffering, but not of sadness. Sadness, she explained, turns you in on yourself and can make you bitter. The Easter perspective of this approach to the experience of the poor is clear, but not everyone achieves it.

In other words, the subject of the mystical dimension in the existence of those who suffer oppression directs us to the situation of the Christian communities that have grown up in what until recently was called the Third World. Their experience of faith is not a simple reflection of what happens where Christianity has been

---

7. See G. Gutiérrez, *A Theology of Liberation* (Maryknoll, N.Y.: Orbis Books, 1988), 106–20; "Liberation, Theology and Proclamation," *Concilium* 6, no. 10 (June 1974): 57–77; "The Poor in the Church," *Concilium* 104 (1977): 11–16.

rooted for many centuries. Forced to adapt to the climate of a different environment and feed on a sap produced by other soil, faith has produced rich fruits with a taste slightly different from that which many people were used to, but does that mean that these fruits are less authentic and nourishing?

The establishment of "winter gardens" to reproduce the European climate in other environments — a practice in which some persist — only leads to artificial situations with no future. The demands of what is today called "inculturation" — something on which the Latin American bishops at their 1992 general conference in Santo Domingo insisted — go beyond adaptation and call for a revision of mental categories. This will not come about without cases of hesitation and misunderstanding, but also not without determination and courage on the part of those who see this change as essential if the Christian faith is to have a vital presence in the world of today.

At a Bound

From being second-class members even of the Christian churches, the oppressed are coming to be full disciples of Jesus. From having their experience of God and their theological reflection underestimated, they are now beginning to enrich the universal Christian community, and this is also happening with the mystical dimension of their faith in a world of poverty, which some mistakenly think leaves no room for gratuitousness or at most summons us to the struggle for justice. The process has been and is long and costly, like that which John describes for us in the supremely important and beautiful ninth chapter of his Gospel.

The story in John 9 introduces us to a person who is clearly, for the evangelist, the model of the disciple. A blind beggar (and so doubly poor) recovers his sight through the action of Jesus. In the sharp dialogues to which this fact gives rise, the former blind man repeats how things happened, how Jesus gave him his sight. What John is doing is insisting on the experience which is at the start of the faith of a person taking the road toward discipleship.

Those who had been accustomed to see the man blind and sitting begging doubt his identity. It can't be the same person: how can this reject possibly now be someone able to see and fend for himself? Those who are insignificant should stay that way; that's how the world is, and any change overturns an order in which everything is in its proper place. We are very familiar with this reaction today as well. There now begins a series of dialogues in which, in a move which is extremely significant and unique in his Gospel, John makes Jesus disappear for twenty-eight whole verses. In his place is none other than the man he has cured and who gradually adopts the status of disciple: the evangelist even puts into his mouth an expression he usually keeps for the Lord: "I am he" (literally, "I am," 9:9). His experience leads him to a simple affirmation, to a first step in his journey as a disciple: he received his sight from "the man called Jesus" (9:11).

However, the doubts of the man's neighbors are nothing to the aggressiveness the incident provoked in the powerful. The Pharisees believe he was never blind, and that they are faced, not with mistaken identity, but with a deliberate lie: this Jesus cannot have done this. The former blind man does not stop at describing what happened: without fear he goes up another rung and tells the élite of his people that the person who did this "is a prophet" (9:17).

The dialogue — the dispute — begins to take on a theological flavor. Arguing from their abstract principles, the experts in the Law insist that this Jesus is a sinner and cannot have done what the accused—as he increasingly is—claims. The man starts from his experience and grows in his convictions: "Do you also want to become his disciples?" he asks ironically (9:27). He is now arguing equal to equal with those who claimed a religious and theological superiority, with those who assumed they knew all about God, and refutes them when he maintains — to the surprise and opposition of the great of his world — that if Jesus "were not from God, he could do nothing" (9:33).

The author of the Gospel now brings Jesus back. With the experience not just of being healed, but also of meeting Jesus, the new disciple realizes what he now can see and confesses without fear, "Lord, I believe" (9:38). The light of faith has opened his eyes a second time and radically changed his life. From being excluded, insignificant, and despised, he has come to be a disciple, to take Christ's place in the story, to confound those who prided themselves on their knowledge.

This maturation of faith ought to overcome the skepticism of those accustomed to a particular social or religious system, enable them to resist the onslaught of the powerful, to stand up to the pride of those who think they have nothing to learn, to talk on an equal footing to those who boast of an alleged superiority. In a sense the poor and oppressed peoples who have made the Christian faith their own are represented by this beggar blind from birth. Many would have preferred to see them always subject to charity, unable to stand up for themselves and to think out in original ways their path as disciples of Jesus. Of all the Lord's disciples—John likes to call them friends—the man blind from birth is the evangelist's favorite, who, like the poor of this world, has no name. His passage through history and his becoming a disciple is bringing them out of anonymity. Their experience of God, the mystical dimension of their lives, does not appear at the end of the road; it grows little by little out of their state of exclusion and oppression.

The Synoptic Gospels, in accounts that are less detailed but no less significant, give us a similar message in the story of the blind man of Jericho. At the exit from the city a sightless beggar (doubly poor, once more) is sitting by the edge of the road. As Jesus comes by, this man who sees what others are unable to see, shouts out "son of David" and asks him for help (Mark 10:47).

The God of Jesus is none other than the God of the forgotten and excluded, of those who people want to silence, which in this case was the action of the people around the Lord (see Mark 10:48). But Jesus has come for these first, and the prospect of the death he will face very soon in Jerusalem does not prevent him from having time for the suffering and the hope of this poor man. He asks him to come near, and the blind man does so, according to the text, "with a bound" (see 10:50), perhaps over the heads of those who were demanding that he be silent.

Jesus does not impose his power on him, does not claim to know what he wants, does not overwhelm him with his help; he

asks, "What do you want me to do for you?" (10:51). Listening is
an important element of dialogue, and in this case the Lord makes
a space for the beggar to take an initiative and assert himself as
a person. The poor are not objects of favor; they are subjects of
rights and desires. When the man asks Jesus to make him see, Jesus
observes that the blind man has taken an active part in this event:
"your faith has made you well" (10:52). At that moment Barti-
maeus—this time we know his name—gets up, leaves the side of
the road, and sets foot on it, following Jesus as a disciple.

The processes recorded are significant and paradigmatic. The
call to discipleship is permanent and includes in a special way the
forgotten and oppressed. The Bartimaeuses of this world have
stopped being at the side of the road; they have jumped up and
come to the Lord, their lifelong friend. Their presence may up-
set the old followers of Jesus, who spontaneously, and with the
best reasons in the world, begin to defend their privileges. They
have discovered—and it cost them an effort to do so—*one* way
of being a Christian, and no doubt they think it is *the* way to be a
Christian for everyone. This sometimes throws up novel demands
for proper conduct in life and in Christian thinking which are not
confined to the offices of some Church authorities; they are also
the result of the exegesis and theology done in the North Atlantic
world and even extend to ordinary Christians in those latitudes.
They frequently react to the eleventh-hour disciples (workers)
with the "envy" the Gospel describes (Matt. 20:1–16, esp. 15).
Clearly the gratuitousness of God's love challenges the patterns
we have become used to.

A Theocentric Option

What is fundamental to the theological experience and reflection that has taken place in Latin America in recent decades is
summed up in what we call the preferential option for the poor.
The idea — and the phrase — has succeeded in piercing layers
of initial resistance and hostility until it finally penetrated the
universal magisterium of the Church. But there is still a long
way to go.

The preferential option came into being in the context of a historical event of vast proportions which we know as the entry of the poor onto the stage of history. This phenomenon takes various forms across the planet. This situation has forced before our eyes with stark clarity the ancient and cruel poverty of the great majority of the world's population, which as come onto the stage of society — as Las Casas said of the Indian nations of his time — with their poverty on their backs. But this situation has also brought into play the energies and qualities of this people. It is a phenomenon not without ambivalences, but challenging and in many respects full of promise, as it has enabled the poor and oppressed to begin to feel in control of their own history, like people at last holding the reins of their own destiny.

These events revived discussion about poverty in the Church, and sent it in new directions. So in Latin America, since July 1967, a distinction has been made between three senses of "poverty": real (or material) poverty, which is an evil; spiritual poverty in the sense of spiritual childhood, surrender of our lives to God's will; and poverty as solidarity with the poor and protest against the situation in which they live. This emphasis implies a particular analysis of poverty and its causes and also presupposes biblical basis both for the rejection of this inhuman situation and of the way spiritual poverty is understood. Finally it clarifies the reasons — which have nothing to do with any sort of idealism — for Christian commitment in this field.

This impulse was welcomed a year later at the Latin American bishops' conference at Medellín (1968) and gave clarity to a commitment which many were beginning to make. Then, between Medellín and the next conference at Puebla (1979), this distinction gave rise, within the Christian communities, to the expression "preferential (spiritual poverty), option (solidarity and protest) for the poor (real poverty)." This option became a cornerstone for the Church's pastoral action, and an important standard for a way of being Christian, that is, for what we call a spirituality.

The truth is that the ultimate reason for preferring the poor and oppressed does not lie in the social analysis we employ, in our human compassion, or in the direct contact we may have with the world of poverty. All these are valid motives, important factors in this commitment, but this option has its real roots in the experience of the gratuitousness of God's love, in faith in the God of life who rejects the unjust and early death which is what poverty means. It is a theocentric option, based on the practice of solidarity and the practice of prayer among us. It is a gift and a task.

The preferential option for the poor is much more than a way of showing our concern about poverty and the establishment of justice. Inevitably, at its very heart, it contains a spiritual, mystical element, an experience of gratuitousness that gives it depth and fruitfulness.[8] This is not to deny the social concern expressed in this solidarity, the rejection of injustice and oppression that it implies, but to see that in the last resort it is anchored in our faith in the God of Jesus Christ. It is therefore not surprising that this option has been adorned by the martyr's witness of so many, as it has by the daily generous self-sacrifice of so many more — ignored by the mass media — who by coming close to the poor set foot on the path to holiness.

The answer to the question about the nature of the mystical dimension in the faith-life of an oppressed person involves understanding the meaning of the preferential option for the poor. And this in turn cannot be seen in its full scope until we become aware of the inculturation of the Christian faith in nations that are poor but rich through a cultural and historical journey different and distant from those of the North Atlantic world.

Faith in the risen Christ is nourished by the experience of suffering, of death, and also of hope among the poor and oppressed, by their way of relating to each other and to nature, by their cultural and religious expressions. Asserting one's own characteristics does not mean refusing to learn, to be enriched by, to open oneself to, other perspectives. It means rather staying alive to be able to receive and grow. Going to the roots ensures creativity, renews

---

8. This is what makes us sensitive to the discourses of justice and gratuitousness that the writer of the book of Job uses to talk about God. See the studies by L. Alonso Schökel subsequently collected in his *Job: Comentario teológico y literario* (Madrid: Cristiandad, 1983); the excellent article by W. Vogele, "Job a parlé correctement," *Nouvelle Revue Théologique* (November–December 1980): 835–52, and G. Gutiérrez, *On Job: God Talk and the Suffering of the Innocent* (Maryknoll, N.Y.: Orbis Books, 1987).

the tree. At the heart of a situation that excludes them and strips them of everything, and from which they seek to free themselves, the poor and oppressed believe in the God of life. Rilke was right when he said that God is in the roots.

— Translated by Francis McDonagh

– 10 –

The Task of Theology and Ecclesial Experience

I have been asked for a personal statement about the task of theology in relation to the basic ecclesial communities. As I am offering my personal experience, I shall speak, at least partly, in the first person. This makes it a more difficult undertaking than a purely abstract treatment of the subject would be. It is also difficult because I am uncertain where to begin. I will try one approach, well aware that there are others.

Questions of Method

During my years as a university student and as a member of lay apostolic groups, I, like my friends, was anxious to acquire a fuller and better knowledge of Christian doctrine. This was what we called the aspect of study or formation, which we saw as a necessary condition for action, in accordance with the famous principle expressed in the demanding formula: "No one can give what they do not have." This study consisted in obligatory but brief biblical commentary, the analysis of encyclicals, both about social matters (*Rerum Novarum, Quadragesimo Anno*) and more strictly doctrinal ones (*Mediator Dei, Mystici Corporis*), and some occasional — often unfinished — reading of authors such as R. Guardini, K. Adam, etc.

In those days the term "theology" was unfamiliar to us, and we thought of it as existing on some high, unattainable plane.

Published in Leonardo Boff and Virgil Elizondo, eds., *La Iglesia Popular: Between Fear and Hope,* Concilium 176 (1984).

According to a well-known priest, perhaps we always associated theology with German names and the German language, which only increased our feeling of the distance between us and what we considered a matter for specialists.

Later, as a first year theology student trying to assimilate Peruvian and Latin American literature and experience, one subject interested me above all: the introduction to theology. The question of the meaning and function of our understanding of the faith in Christian and ecclesial life seemed to me not only to come before any other question but also to be *the* central and decisive question, as well as always remaining an open one. I was passionately devoted to the study of the first question in St. Thomas Aquinas's *Summa Theologica,* Melchior Cano's contribution to the places for theology (*loci theologici*), and the classic book by Gardeil on these issues. Over several vacations I devoured the article "Theology" by Y. Congar (in the *Dictionary of Catholic Theology*). His historical perspective got me out of an almost exclusively rational way of looking at theological work. It opened my mind to other ways of seeing (that of the Tübingen School, for example). A discreet contact with the book by M. D. Chenu *The Saulchoir School* revealed the whole scope of human history to me and the life of the Church itself as a place for theology.

One result of this interest was that in the theological treatises I read afterward I paid close attention to the methodological aspect and to the relation between theology and the sources of revelation. Many of my professors helped in this by their insistence on the Bible.

As a student, one of the things I tried to do was to deepen my own knowledge, so that later I could teach this aspect of theology, as it seemed to me a useful way of situating theology's why and wherefore. However, I never did get to teach theology regularly in a faculty of theology, at least not in my own country. I was confined to giving theology courses — from which in fact I benefited greatly — to students in other faculties, which meant that the presentation had to be less specialized and within the broad scope of the relation between faith and culture.

In fact, as a priest, my whole time was taken up by pastoral work, which I enjoyed very much. At first I worked with university students, and then, through this work, I came more and more into contact with the working class and the poor, until a certain fusion took place between these two mutually challenging and complementary pastoral areas. Thus I was led by events to a way of doing theology which I had not foreseen in my student years.

The Subject of Theology

The poor with their deprivation and their richness burst into my life. This is a people suffering from injustice and exploitation but whose faith at the same time goes very deep. Work with what could generally be called basic ecclesial communities, a term expressing this entry of the poor into the Church, placed me in contact with a world in which, in spite of its being a reencounter with my own roots, I feel I am merely taking my first steps. Moreover, as time passes I see that the advances I have made are even more timid than I thought a few years ago.

Working in this world and becoming familiar with it, I came to realize, together with others, that the first thing to do is listen. Listen endlessly to the human and religious experiences of those who have made the sufferings, hopes, and struggles of this people their own. Listen, not condescendingly, but to learn about the people and to learn about God. The lesson learned is simple: in the dialogue of a Christian community there is no account of experience without there being an element of reflection, a way of seeing life and faith, contained in it. In what is called life reviewing—a method adopted by many communities—the perspective of faith does not appear only when the effort is made to understand certain experiences in the light of a biblical text. Life in the community means faith translated into active involvement, hope expressed in a particular attitude to life. Reflection on faith can and should expressly try to go deeper, but it also accompanies all Christian activity within a people struggling to affirm their human dignity and their condition as children of God. Sometimes, as well as talk there is also writing about an experience of God, which has become prayer and reflection. It is impossible to do theology from the standpoint of our world without taking into account these testimonies, which are becoming more abundant every day.

This way of working led us to discover — and Puebla recognized this strongly — the "evangelizing power of the poor." This capacity possessed by the poor to be the subject of the Gospel message carries with it a "theologizing" potential. These are not empty words or an attempt at artificial symmetry. It is a challenging daily experience which reformulates the whole question of what theology should be doing. Perhaps it makes us return to the sources, to the first efforts to understand faith in the Church's life, in the service of its task of proclaiming the Gospel, together with those whose function is to lead it by their pastoral and magisterial ministry.

It seemed clear to me that this reflection by communities who evangelize — i.e., proclaim the Gospel — and who are called together as a Church (*ecclesia:* and that is precisely why they are "ecclesial") is doing theology, thinking about the faith, the Christian condition. This is the exercise of the right to think possessed by the poor. It is a means of affirming their right to life, a right that in many different ways they are denied. The faith of the poor needs to understand itself, for its own sake. Fundamentally, this is an expression of the traditional principle "fides quaerens intellectum." The true subject of this reflection is not the isolated theologian, but the Christian community and, rippling out in concentric circles, the whole Church with its different charismata and responsibilities.

Those Christians whom we call theologians in the stricter sense ("professional theologians," as they are called in some places) will do their work effectively to the extent that they are linked to the Christian community, of which they are part and in which they daily share with others the reasons for their hope. It is definitely not a matter of being present to receive the questions asked by the poor and those involved with them in order to answer them on our own account. The task is more complex. Sharing these reflections teaches us that they contain not only questions but also answers, which these Christians are discovering for themselves, to the challenges they face in their solidarity with the poor and oppressed. Liberation theology has to deal with many expressions and categories which come from the basic communities (one of them, for example, is that we mentioned earlier, the evangelizing power of the poor).

Thus the task of the theologian is to contribute to the community what an academic education could have given it in the way of a better knowledge of and familiarity with Holy Scripture, the tradition and teaching of the Church, and contemporary theology. Theology is not an individual task; it is an ecclesial function. It is done from the Word of God received and experienced in the Church, and for the sake of its proclamation to every human being and especially the disinherited of this world. I believe that the need for solidarity with the struggle of the poor to construct a free and just human society and to proclaim the Gospel in the heart of our understanding of the faith, is not merely a necessary condition for what is sometimes called "committed theology." I also think it is necessary — although this is sometimes overlooked — in order to achieve a discourse on the faith which deals with the true and most vital questions for the modern world, in which the basic communities live and bear witness. Finally, it is the necessary condition for the creation of a serious, scientific, and responsible theology.

In fact, contrary to what some people think and fear, experience shows that closeness to the basic communities enforces a strict rigor upon the task of theology. The questions and the broad lines of response which come from them, their requirements for action, their work in the popular environment to which they belong, leave no room for evasive or irresponsible burbling. They require theology which is committed both to the place and to making sense of a — very necessary — reflection upon the faith.

Life and Reflection

Theology understood thus is not free from tensions. For example, how to reconcile belonging to a community with its daily demands with intellectual work which also has its laws and requires its own space and time? How can one undertake a laborious effort to understand the faith when the poor face immediate needs necessary to their physical survival, with all that this implies for their lives as Christians? These questions arise and must be coped with every day.

If we are frank, we have to admit that these questions remain open. We do not manage to solve them satisfactorily; we know, for one thing, that we cannot surrender either side. Anyway, despite everything, does it really matter whether we reach a definitive answer to such questions? Is this not precisely a tension which sets up a discourse on the faith which is really helpful to the Church's work for preaching the Gospel — in word and deed? Might the anxiety that such tension sometimes produces not be a result of the uneasiness felt by the theologian who feels torn in half, although this state is a necessity both for theology itself and, more importantly, for the Christian community within which and for whose sake this intellectual work is done at all?

Neither can these questions be given a peremptory answer. Perhaps they will gradually resolve themselves — or disappear — on the way. It is a different way from the one we foresaw, when as students we felt we had a vocation to do theology. But it keeps what is good in the old way, values what we learn on our journey, and shows us ancient anxieties in a new perspective. Thus we seek and make a language about God (that is, a theology) together with a people living the faith in the midst of a situation of injustice and exploitation which is a denial of God. Their sufferings are accompanied by an unquenchable hope of joy and by love in solidarity with society's poorest and most deprived. It is a contemplative language whose starting point is prayerful silence in the presence of God's mystery. It is a prophetic language which sees Christ as the unbreakable link between the kingdom and the disinherited of this world. It is a language sprouting in the popular sectors of Latin America and other continents, as in the book of Job, from the experience of innocent suffering. It is a voice which has the right to be heard, among others, within the universal Church. A theology seeking to become a hermeneutic of the hope of the poor in the God of life.

There are many methodological points needing critical determination if we are not to become trapped in superficial enthusiasm and facile formulas. But we are convinced that something profound is happening, pregnant with consequences. Only through the following of Jesus, through spirituality, is it possible to create a fruitful discourse on the faith. In it we seek a way to the Father, life in accordance with the Spirit. It is a path beaten by utter faithfulness to the demands of the poor people's world and to the Church called to proclaim the Lord's resurrection, a message of abundant life in the midst of the death to which the poor are condemned. It is a way of living and thinking about the faith in relation to what John XXIII called the Church which belongs to all, and in particular, the Church of the poor.

— *Translated by Dinah Livingstone*

– 11 –

Theology
An Ecclesial Function

I would like to present here some thoughts about how I see the present role and future tasks of theological reflection in the life of the Church present in Latin America and the Caribbean. My intention is to elucidate what I have stated on other occasions and thus to clarify certain concepts in a sphere where it is easy to fall into oversimplifications and even erroneous ways of understanding theological work. The role of theology is not in fact to forge an ideology which would justify social and political positions already taken but rather to help believers to let themselves be judged by the Word of the Lord. Theology cannot therefore give up the critical function of faith vis-à-vis every historical realization. I begin from the conviction that the theological task is a vocation which arises and is exercised in the heart of the ecclesial community. Indeed, its starting point is the gift of faith in which we welcome the truth of the Word of God, and its contributions are at the service of the evangelizing mission of the Church.

This ecclesial location gives theology its raison d'être, determines its scope, nurtures it with the sources of revelation — Scripture and Tradition — enriches it with the recognition of the charisma of the magisterium and dialogue with the magisterium, and puts it in contact with other ecclesial functions.

Published in *Páginas* 130 (1994): 10–17. Translation published in James B. Nickoloff, ed., *Gustavo Gutiérrez: Essential Writings* (Maryknoll, N.Y.: Orbis Books, 1996).

Evangelization and Theology

What is the role of theology in the evangelizing responsibility which is incumbent upon the whole Church? "Theology," says the "Instruction on the Ecclesial Vocation of the Theologian" of the Congregation for the Doctrine of the Faith, "makes its contribution so that faith may be communicable to Christians, of course — thus theology plays an important role within the Church — but also (and in a special way) to "those who do not yet know Christ." The missionary perspective, anxious about the aspirations and concerns of those who are far from, or do not share, the Christian faith, gives the deepest meaning to the effort to understand faith.

Within this dynamism — the dynamism of a "truth which tends toward being communicated" — lies the theological task. Theology is a task carried out in the Church convoked by the Word. From *there,* from "within the Church" (as the Instruction puts it) the truth which frees (see John 8:32) is proclaimed — salvation in Jesus Christ — and theological reflection is carried out. This is what the Latin American bishops called "the prophetic ministry of the Church" when they gathered in Santo Domingo in 1992: to this ministry belongs the service which theologians must offer (33). Its content is the proclamation of Christ and of his integral liberation, the proclamation which must be made in a language faithful to the message and which can speak to our contemporaries. This is the very point of the theological contribution: this is why it must enter into dialogue with the mentality of the culture of those who listen to the Word. In this way it will be able to contribute efficaciously to a pastoral practice which motivates those to whom it is directed to follow the witness and teachings of Jesus.

In this task "the theologian, without ever forgetting that he or she is a member of the People of God, must respect it and commit himself or herself to give them a teaching which does not injure in any way the doctrine of the faith." Otherwise theologians run the risk that the pressing needs of the moment may make it hard to see the requirements of the message in its entirety. They will not fulfill their function of service to the evangelizing of the Church and its pastors. Indeed, "the freedom proper to theological reflection is exercised within the faith of the Church."

Theology is a speaking about God in the light of faith, a language about one who is, in truth, its only theme. We ought to approach the mystery of God with respect and humility; but in a biblical perspective, mystery does not signify something which should remain secret. Rather, mystery should be spoken and communicated. To be revealed belongs to the very essence of mystery (see Rom. 16:25–26). Theology, then, becomes a "science of Christian revelation."

At the same time theologians must be aware that their efforts cannot exhaust the significance of the Word contained in Scripture and transmitted by the living tradition of the Church in which the charisma of the magisterium is located. Furthermore, "the deposit of faith" present in the Church is not limited to answering our queries; it also raises new questions and constantly requires of us an examination of our faith. On the other hand, speaking about God takes place in a constantly changing historical reality in which the ecclesial community lives. No dimension of human existence — which itself is lived in the midst of complex social situations — escapes the condition of being a disciple of Jesus. From this reality arise constant challenges to the discourse on faith. For this reason, the episcopal conference at Santo Domingo — locating itself in its own Latin American environment — speaks of a theological labor which would promote "work in favor of social justice, human rights, and solidarity with the poorest" (33). These are urgent necessities among us.

For these reasons theological language contains much that is approximate: it must therefore always be open to renovation from new perspectives, further precision of concepts, and the correction of formulations. Similarly, there is the permanent emergence of new paths in our speech about God which seeks to express revealed truth in appropriate terms. All this is required along with the clear conviction that — according to a traditional affirmation — no theology can be identified with the faith. Theological pluralism within the unity of faith is an old fact in the Church. In this context different theologies are useful and important efforts but on condition that they do not consider themselves unique or indispensable and that they be aware of their role of modestly serving the primary tasks of the Church.

A Moment for Latin America

When Christian faith, received and lived out in the Church, experiences new challenges to its communication to others, theology asks itself (as it is always called to do) about the relevance of its reflection on the revealed message. There are numerous historical witnesses to this fact. It is the moment to renew this reflection, going once again to the inexhaustible sources of faith which feed the life of the Church.

Poverty is a theme of the Gospels and a challenge which has always been present throughout the Church's history. But the denunciations of Medellín ("inhuman misery"), Puebla ("poverty opposed to the Gospel"), and Santo Domingo ("intolerable extremes of misery"), made the situation of poverty which the great majority of the population of Latin America and the Caribbean suffers appear in all its harshness before our eyes. It was a matter of an age-old reality but one that pounded the human and Christian conscience in a new way and that for the same reason raised demanding questions for the ecclesial task. The "others" of a society which marginalizes and excludes them became present, demanding solidarity. The root question — how to say to the poor, to the least of society, that God loves them? — has demonstrated its fruitfulness in the pastoral action of the Church and in the theological path undertaken to respond to it.

In the face of unjust and premature death which poverty implies, "the noble combat for justice" (Pius XII) acquires dramatic and urgent characteristics. To be aware of this is a question of clarity and honesty. It is necessary, moreover, to overcome the mentality which places these facts in an exclusively political field in which faith has little or nothing to say; this attitude expresses the "divorce between faith and life" which Santo Domingo sees still today as capable of "producing clamorous situations of injustice, social inequality, and violence" (24). However, to recognize social conflicts as a fact must not in any way signify that social conflict is being promoted as a method of change in society. Thus we cannot accept "the programmed class struggle" (John Paul II, *Laborem Exercens, II*).

We are without a doubt on controversial and slippery terrain. The risk of reductionism (or of expressions which can be interpreted as reductionistic) is thus limiting and threatening. It is easy to be absorbed by the emotional aspects of the situation, to experience a certain fascination with something new, or to overestimate the value of the social sciences. The social sciences are necessary if we are to understand socioeconomic reality, but they represent efforts still in the beginning stages. In view of this to speak of a scientific understanding of the social universe cannot be considered something definite or apodictic, nor as something completely free of ideological connections.

As for the distinction among three levels in the notion of liberation, Puebla therefore alerts us that "the unity of these three planes" implies that "the mystery of the death and resurrection of Jesus Christ must be lived out on the three planes...without making any one of them exclusive" (326). This is the integral liberation in Christ which leads us to full communion with God and others (see LG 1). Social and political liberation should not in any way hide the final and radical significance of liberation from sin which can only be a work of forgiveness and of God's grace. It is important then to refine our means of expression in order to avoid confusion in this matter.

We must pay attention to these dangers and reaffirm the proper and direct level of the Gospel; its content is the reign, but the reign must be accepted by people who live in history and consequently the proclamation of a reign of love, peace, and justice impinges on life together in society. Nevertheless, the demands of the Gospel go beyond the political project of building a different society. Society will be just, and in a certain sense new, to the degree that it places the dignity of the human person at its center — a dignity that for a Christian has its ultimate foundation in the condition of being the "image of God" which Christ saves by reestablishing the friendship between human beings and God.

Conflictive social realities cannot make us forget the requirements of a universal love that does not recognize boundaries of social class, race, or gender. The affirmation that the human person is the agent of his or her own destiny in history must be made in such a way that the gratuitous initiative of God in the salvific process—the ultimate meaning of the historical evolution of humanity—may be clearly seen. Indeed, the gift of God "who loved us first" (1 John 4:19) frames and gives rise to human action as a free response to that love.

It is possible to go astray in these matters, and in fact this has happened. Nor have misunderstandings been lacking in the face of new themes and new languages. In this way a debate over the theology of liberation arose which even flowed beyond the world of the Church and into the wide and stormy world of the media. Nevertheless, beyond appearances and arduous discussions, a profound process was taking place in those years, characterized by a serious and respectful confrontation, well-founded objections, requests for necessary refinements from those who have authority in the Church to do so, recognition of the value of being sensitive to the sign of the times which the aspiration to liberation signifies, a legitimate presentation of doubts, and interest in a theology close to the base Christian communities.

All this leads us to see that the effort to capture new realities theologically has to be constantly clarified. Imperfections of language must be overcome, and inexact formulations must be corrected by concepts which do not give rise to errors in matters concerning the doctrine of the faith. Indeed, theological reflection always carries the imprint of the moment and of the circumstances in which it is formulated. This is true in particular for the effort undertaken in Latin America in these years when it was necessary to confront difficult situations, respond to unheard of challenges to the understanding of the faith, and be able to reach—with the missionary spirit proper to theology—those who do not perceive the significance of the Gospel for these realities and for their lives.

It is important above all to be clear about these risks and limitations, to listen with humility to divergent opinions. This attitude follows—it is appropriate to note it—from understanding the meaning of theological work as a service to the evangelizing mission of the entire Church to which I have already referred. In theology it is necessary to be ever ready, in the words of John Paul II, to "modify one's own opinions" in function of one's service to "the community of believers." This is the meaning of theological works; this is why it may rightly be affirmed, as the "Letter on the Formation of Future Priests" puts it, that theology "cannot prescind from the doctrine and lived experience in the sphere of the Church in which the magisterium authentically watches over and interprets the deposit of faith."

To Proclaim the Reign Today

For all these reasons, and because the process has been complex and difficult but simultaneously rich, a fundamental perspective has opened up a path which carries with it the best of the ecclesial experience of this period. I refer to the preferential option for the poor which, born of the experience and practice of the Latin American Christian communities, was first expressed at Medellín and then explicitly embraced at Puebla. As we know, this focus is today part of the universal magisterium of the Church, as numerous texts of John Paul II and of diverse non–Latin American episcopacies attest. If something should remain from this period of Latin American and Church history, it is precisely this option as a demanding commitment, an expression of a love which is always new, and the axis of a new evangelization of the continent.

A series of economic, political, and ecclesial events, as much worldwide as Latin American or national, make people think that the stage in which the theological reflection recalled a few pages ago came to be born is now coming to an end. The years which have passed were, on the one hand, stimulating and creative, but tense and conflictive on the other. In the face of new situations (the worsening of poverty and the end of certain political projects, for example), many earlier discussions do not respond to current challenges.

Everything would seem to indicate that a different period is beginning. The collaboration of all in facing the enormous questions which the reality of Latin America presents us becomes more and more necessary. There is a reconstitution of the social fabric within which we had sought to place the proclamation of the reign of God, a reconstitution which requires new liberating practices. These must be careful not to fall into the "verticalism of a disembodied spiritual union with God or into a simple existential personalism...nor, even less, into socioeconomic-political horizontalism" (Puebla 329). Both deviations, each in its own way, distort at the same time the transcendence and the immanence of the reign of God.

The summoning tone of the Santo Domingo texts responds to this requirement and thus makes an energetic call to all to participate in the *new evangelization* of the continent. This concern was present since the preparations for Medellín, but it took on new strength with the vigorous call of John Paul II in Haiti (1983), the poorest and most forgotten country of Latin America. Directing himself to CELAM, the pope spoke of "a new evangelization — new in its zeal, in its methods, in its expression." Santo Domingo made this perspective one of its central themes and one of its primary pastoral directions. The theological reflection formulated in the Latin American context finds here fertile ground in its collaboration with the evangelizing task of the Church. Making use of successes and avoiding failures of previous years, our discourse on the faith should help us to find the route and the language to proclaim to "the poor of this continent" the need for the "Gospel of radical and integral liberation"; not to do so, adds John Paul II, would be to cheat and disillusion the poor.

Santo Domingo takes up a second theme from which it deduces an important pastoral direction: *human promotion*. This is not something foreign or extrinsic to evangelization. In recent years numerous texts of the magisterium have vigorously reminded us that to promote human dignity is part of the evangelizing task. It is a dignity called into question by "the most devastating and humiliating scourge which Latin America and the Caribbean are experiencing" and constituted by "the growing impoverishment" of millions of Latin Americans — the consequence in large part of the "policies of the neoliberal type" which predominate on the continent (Santo Domingo 179).

The depth of the problem is such that it calls the entire Church — with no exceptions — to face it. Biblical reflection on poverty and the experiences of solidarity of previous years are of great usefulness here, but this must not hide what is distinct or delicate in the present situation. The renovation of the Church's social teaching energetically undertaken by John Paul II not only offers guidelines for an authentic and contemporary social harmony and for the construction of a just and new society with total respect for human life and dignity, but will also enrich the theological task and provide a fertile field of study pertinent to the social and historical context of Latin America. These texts remind us that the values of peace, justice, and liberty are not only goals of a social commitment but that they ought to inspire, beginning now, the methods we employ for achieving a human society which respects the rights of all.

The new evangelization will have to be an *inculturated evangelization.* "Inculturation" is a new term for designating an old reality which, for the Christian, carries resonances of incarnation. The Word must incarnate itself in diverse worlds, situations, and cultures. Despite this, its transcendence is not affected; rather, it is reaffirmed. This perspective has put a finger right on the wound in a continent of such great racial and cultural diversity. The cultures and values of the different indigenous peoples and of the black population of Latin America constitute a great treasure which must be appreciated and respected by those who have the responsibility for proclaiming the Gospel. We are face to face with an immense and urgent task which has scarcely been initiated and with a stimulating challenge to theological reflection.

These are, then, three themes, three primary pastoral directions (see Santo Domingo, 287–301), and thus three spheres of theological reflection which, as I have pointed out, seek to be at the service of the proclamation of the "Gospel of liberation."

To take up these perspectives is to renew "the evangelical and preferential option for the poor, following the example and the words of the Lord Jesus" (Santo Domingo 180). Christ is, indeed, the ultimate foundation of this option and of the pastoral directions mentioned. As the "living Son of God," he is "the unique reason for our life and the source of our mission" (Santo Domingo 296).

For this reason the preferential option for the poor not only demands that we seek to know, seriously and responsibly, the reality and the causes of poverty: not only does such an option lead us to make our pastoral action more effective and to deepen our theological reflection. It also ought to mark our spirituality — that is, our following of Jesus Christ, who is "the way, the truth, and the life" (John 14:6). His life, his death, and his resurrection put their imprint on the course in history taken by the Church and by every Christian.

Like every believer, the theologian must undertake the discipleship of Jesus. For this purpose, she (or he) will, like Mary, have to preserve "all these things in her heart" (Luke 2:51), that is, the deeds and words in which God is revealed. Whatever the historical context may be in which we live, no matter how tense the situations which must be faced, this discipleship signifies leading a life nourished — as John frequently says — by the will of the Father. The contemplative dimension, the practice of prayer, is essential to the Christian life.

In concrete and beautiful terms Puebla invited us "to discover in the suffering faces of the poor the face of the Lord" (31–39). Santo Domingo reiterates this call and proposes that we extend further the list of those suffering faces who populate our continent (see 178 and 179). This discovery and this solidarity are the privileged way in history by which the Spirit leads us to the Father through Jesus Christ.

— *Translated by James B. Nickoloff*

– 12 –

Theological Language
Fullness of Silence

Theology is a language. It attempts to speak a word about the mysterious reality that believers call God. It is a *logos* about *theos*.

I have said "mysterious reality" and I would like to make it clear that I am taking the word "mystery" in its biblical sense. The French philosopher Gabriel Marcel helped us to understand the matter by drawing a distinction between "problem," "enigma," and "mystery." God is not a problem before which we stand impersonally and that we treat as an object. Nor is God an enigma, something utterly unknown and incomprehensible. In the Bible God is a mystery to the extent that God is an all-enveloping love. In Marcel's terminology, God is the mystery of the Thou that we can only acknowledge and invoke.

Hence — and always speaking from a biblical standpoint — mystery is not ineffable in the literal meaning of the word. It must, with all the proper qualifications, be spoken and communicated. To conceal it, to keep it withdrawn to a private sphere, or to limit it to a few initiates is to ignore its very essence. The mystery of God's love must be proclaimed. Doing so presupposes a language, a means of communication, a language located more in the disturbing certainty of hope than in the serenity brought about by an innocuous knowledge.

Believing is an experience that is both interior and shared in community. Faith is a relationship between persons; that is why

This address was delivered in 1995 on the occasion of the author's induction to the Peruvian Academy of the Spanish Language. Published in *Páginas* 137 (1996): 66–87. Translation published, in part, in James B. Nickoloff, ed., *Gustavo Gutiérrez: Essential Writings* (Maryknoll, N.Y.: Orbis Books, 1996).

we said it is a gift. The mystery of God must be accepted in prayer and in human solidarity; it is the moment of silence and of practice. Within that moment—and only from within it—will there arise the language and the categories necessary for transmitting it to others, for entering into communication, in the strong sense of the term: in communion with those others; that is the moment of speaking.

In a beautiful passage, the Book of Ecclesiastes tells us that throughout human life everything has its moment and season: "a time to be silent and a time to speak" (3:7). These moments are not simply set side by side, but rather one depends on the other, and they nourish one another. Without silence there is no true speaking. In listening and meditation, what is to be spoken begins to be sketched faintly and hesitatingly. Likewise, expressing our inner world will lead us to gain new and fruitful areas of personal silence and encounter. That is what happens in theology.

Keeping in mind these preliminary considerations, I would like to offer some observations on the present situation of theological language, in particular on the connection between theological language and the human condition. Such observations may perhaps help us to appreciate the magnitude of a major development: for some decades now in Latin America and beyond it, a way of speaking of God is stammeringly coming to birth, a way of speaking marked by the cultural diversity of humankind and the conditions created by poverty and marginalization. This will be our subject in the following pages. The questions that arise from the historical use of that theological language, its simultaneous particularity and universality, and finally the narrative dimension of the life and teachings of Jesus of Nazareth, will help us to approach it.

The Sick and Healing God

It is not enough to say that the word about God is born of the need to formulate and communicate an experience of belief. Belief comes in the context of living human experience, with all its challenging complexity. A whole social and cultural world is involved in the development of theological language. The questions that arise from situations of human extremity cut deep; the appeal cuts through anecdotal and passing experience to the essence. These questions leave us naked before the basic inquiry of all human beings. If we don't go down or rather up into the world of everyday suffering, of consuming anguish, of ever-burning hope, the theological task has no substance. Two writers will help give flesh — wounded flesh — to this challenge as we see it today.

Walking with the Poor

Felipe Guamán Poma lives in his own mental universe; this sometimes makes it difficult for unwary readers, especially if they are excessively marked by a Western perspective and logic. He writes his long report to the king of Spain as an Indian, a member of a people whose tribulations he seeks to denounce and whose rights he seeks to defend. He also writes as a new Christian, making the life of Jesus with his preferential love for the poor the fundamental criterion by which to discern justice and injustice in the Peruvian Andes.

Having walked nameless for thirty years in the midst of the abused and neglected Indians, he can speak at first hand of the abuse they receive. His denunciation is anchored in painful experience. The old cliché with which he ends his painful descriptions, "nothing can be done," shows dramatically that what he has seen and heard has carried him to the edge of despair. His cry and his call come from there. Seeing how as he writes in faltering and apparently disordered Spanish "the poor ones of Christ are canceled out and used," he exclaims: "and so my God, where are you? Can't you hear me to remedy your poor ones, because I am full to remedy."[1] Reproachfulness struggles to be heard in his cry, just as when Job says in the Bible, after a heartrending depiction of the situation of the poor, "yet God pays no attention to their prayer" (Job 24:12).

Guamán Poma forces us to hit bottom. This is a question born of the suffering of the innocent, of what A. Gesché calls "evil

1. *Primer nueva corónica y buen gobierno* (Mexico City: Siglo XXI, 1980), 1104.

misfortune" as distinguished from "culpable evil."[2] But the question also grows out of the experience of faith. For those who are raising it today, "faith is precisely the reason for perplexity" as South African Archbishop Desmond Tutu, a great witness of our time, has said in a similar context.[3] Indeed God's silence is even more unbearable for those who believe that the God of their faith is the God of life and love.

Guamán Poma does not stop there. His reflection goes deeper; from the heights of the Andes he sketches out a language about God which he sees as valid "for all the world and Christendom."[4] The suffering of the poor helps him rediscover, and explain in his way, a profound Christian insight: "the rich and proud for them devalue the poor, thinking that where the poor are, there is no God and justice. So with faith they must know clearly that where the poor are, there is Jesus Christ himself, where God is, there is justice."[5] Behind that affirmation, upholding it, is the message of the biblical prophets and Jesus himself (see Matt. 25:31–46).

The theological language of Guamán Poma stands in the paradox, almost the contradiction, between the anguished question: "My God, where are you? Can't you hear me?" and the nonetheless hoped-for recognition of God's presence in the abandoned and mistreated people of this world. His God-talk does not drown its voice in the intimacy of a painful experience; still less is it limited to declarations of principle. It conveys demands for everyday behavior. Our author understands that, and writes his text to stop the devaluation and persecution of "the poor ones of Jesus Christ."[6] For him, "to serve God as our Lord and to favor the poor ones of Jesus Christ" are inseparable dimensions of Christian practice.[7]

---

2. "Le problème du mal, problème de société" in *Théologie de la libération* (Louvain, 1985).

3. "The Theology of Liberation in Africa," in *African Theology en route* (Maryknoll, N.Y.: Orbis Books, 1979), 163.

4. Guamán Poma, *Primer nueva corónica*, 1168.

5. Ibid.

6. Ibid., 903.

7. Ibid., 1105.

The Liberating God

Centuries later José María Arguedas, another "sentencer by eyes and by sight," as Guamán Poma called himself, called attention to the persistent and increasing suffering of a marginalized people. This time religion was apparently aggravating that unjust pain. In the cathedral of Cusco the young Ernesto, Arguedas's alter ego, says in consternation about the Lord of the earthquakes: "raging, sorrowing, the Lord had a silence that did not calm, that caused suffering. . . . The face of Christ created suffering, spread it out to the walls, to the vaults and columns. I expected tears to fall from them."[8] These are tears that provoke, and seek to justify, other tears that are shed by those who see their human dignity trampled upon. He suffered and he caused suffering. The beauty of that expression underlines an ancient, cruel, and profound reality.

A religion that saddens and does not try, as it should, to help the heart grow in joy and hope plunges the poor back into their misery and their needs. What most exasperates Arguedas is that it makes others suffer; nothing is dirtier than that. And we know how important the categories of purity and dirtiness were to Arguedas.

None of us have described with such empathy and mastery the everyday pain and the inexhaustible energy of a historically neglected people. But more than that, in the face of the suffering Christ Arguedas sees the features of the houseboy, the Indian humiliated and abused by the sinister character called El Viejo who represents the Antichrist. The resemblance between the crucified one and the houseboy reinforces a theme commonly found in the theology that is being developed today in Latin America: the poor are a crucified people.[9] It is impossible to live and think about the faith without keeping this situation in mind. That was also the evangelical insight of Bartolomé de Las Casas when he affirmed, speaking of the indigenous population in the Indies, that

---

8. *Los ríos profundos,* in J. M. Arguedas, *Obras completas* (Lima: Editorial Horizonte, 1983), 3:24.

9. See I. Ellacuría, "El pueblo crucificado," in *Cruz y Resurrección* (Mexico City: CRT, 1978), 48.

he had left "Jesus Christ, our God, whipped, smitten, slapped, and crucified, not once but thousands of times."[10]

Because some religious interpretations justify and others reject the oppression of the poor, a character in *Todas las sangres* asks in annoyance: "how many Jesus Christs are there?" More than an expression of skepticism and detachment, this is a natural demand for explanation and clarification. A few lines later comes the terrible discovery: "The God of the nobility is different. He causes suffering without consolation." The fine and tender poet Gonzalo Rose once said of the God who causes suffering, "That's not our God, is it, Mamá?"[11]

The line about the God of the nobility is at the heart of a dialogue between a priest and a mestizo sacristan who speaks for Arguedas. In the writer's personal copy of this novel we find the following marginal note, handwritten beside the dialogue: "This is the greatest novel of the Andean world written in the colonial period."[12] This clearly shows the importance that Arguedas attributed to his own text on rereading it.

Once more a heartbreakingly unjust condition, and perplexity in the face of human sorrow, take us to the depths without diversion or mitigation, reopening a possibility and a method of God-talk. But Arguedas was not only able to depict the piercing sorrow of a people; he was also attentive to their simple hopes and everyday joys. Thus shortly before his own tragic death, he wrote to a friend that recently "my faith in the future, which has never failed me, has been strengthened. How well we understand each other, and together see the light that no one can darken!"[13] The life that breathes in this text stands in apparent, or real, opposition to what was about to happen.

Falteringly, with uncertain steps, from an experience that weaves together anguish and hope, sorrow and joy, tribulations and assurance, Arguedas goes more and more deeply into the enormous and complex reality that he wants to express and trans-

---

10. *Historia de las Indias,* in *Obras Escogidas* (Madrid: BAE, 1957), 2:511.
11. "La pregunta" in *Hallazgos y extravíos* (Mexico City: FCE, 1968), 30.
12. Reproduced in *Obras Completas,* 4:457.
13. Quoted in G. Gutiérrez, *Entre las calandrias* (Lima: CEP-IBC, 1990), 24.

192 • Spirituality and Theology

form. At times he seems to feel that something has come back into the experience of the people with whom he has cast his lot, and into his own experience. He calls it the liberating God, the One whom the mestizo sacristan, like Guamán Poma and with good reason, declares absent wherever injustice rules.[14]

How far does Arguedas's last insight take him? It is hard to say; besides, there are personal thresholds that no one else can cross, an intimate world that must be respected. For our purposes it is enough to say that he has fully raised the question. The human density expressed in the question is an inescapable challenge to all God-talk, however José María may have answered it at the end.

Absence and Presence

Attention to human suffering at the personal and social levels, to poverty and marginalization, keeps us, as Arguedas puts it, from "swimming in the rubble of this nation."[15] What is secondary and superficial evaporates, ideological and religious options lose their relevance, and one's place of birth, social class, and race hardly matter. Human suffering, which Arguedas likens to the sound of María Angola, penetrates the human being with such weight that one cries out like César Vallejo: "today I only suffer."[16] From its long experience, a whole people can say with the poet:

> I was born one day
> when God was sick,
> very sick.[17]

This is an echo of the biblical lament of Job: "Let the day perish in which I was born. . . . Let it not rejoice among the days of the year; let it not come into the number of the months" (Job 3:2–6). He tries in vain to turn back the hands of the clock, to return to the time before his birth, to tear out that day from the calendar and thus wipe out his suffering at its roots.

---

14. See ¿Ultimo diario? in Obras completas, 5:198.
15. El Zorro de arriba y el zorro de abajo in Obras completas, 5:178.
16. "Voy a hablar de la esperanza," in Poemas en prosa.
17. "Espergia" in Heraldos negros.

But we must not forget that for Vallejo that sick God is also a solicitous healer who seeks to alleviate the pain:

> And God hastens to take
> the pulse, gravely, silently,
> and like a father tending his child,
> slightly,
> ever so slightly lifts the bloody bandage
> and holds hope between his fingers.[18]

Hope born in the midst of affliction, hope moistened by tears and blood, but real and vital hope nonetheless. A sick God, absent and deaf, and yet a healing God, concerned and tender. Here is a dialectical, and therefore fruitful, approach to a necessarily equivocal reality.

There is no greater challenge to our language about God than the suffering of the innocent. How can we understand a God of love in a world that bears the stamp of poverty, genocide, terrorist violence, disregard for the most elemental human rights? It is that simple and urgent. This question is surely broader than any answer theology can give. But it is an inescapable question. After the Holocaust Emmanuel Lévinas insightfully developed an ethic of the other, holding up the face of someone who says "don't kill me!" and thinking of God as Otherness.[19] Poverty and its consequences are the great challenge of our time. Poverty which in the last analysis means early and unjust death, destroying persons, families, and nations. Indeed poverty cannot be reduced to the social and economic sphere; it is a global human problem.

Should we call this a precritical position on the problem? Now is not the time to debate that point in detail, or to challenge the axiomatic way that this observation has been presented in the context of the Enlightenment and of a critical reasoning that constantly chases its own tail. I will simply say that our discourse on God cannot be separated from the everyday life of the poor of

---

18. *Trilce* XXXI.
19. E. Lévinas, *Totalité et Infini* (The Hague: Martinus Nijhoff, 1968). See the observations of D. Tracy, "Evil, Suffering, Hope: The Search for New Forms of Contemporary Theodicy" (unpublished, June 1995).

this world, a life infused with sorrow and hope. The experience of hunger and oppression changes our God-talk. Indeed all that is truly human must be reflected in that language. The German theologian Karl Rahner has said that in our time reality is struggling for a chance to speak. Theology should be in the midst of that struggle; it cannot stand off at a dead point of history, watching it pass. If it is not about the complex goings and comings of human existence, language about God would be like the tennis game without a ball in one of Antonioni's films.

A theological language that does not reject unjust suffering, that does not speak out loud about the right of all to be happy, betrays the God of whom we speak. The creation story in Genesis, the book of beginnings, tells us that at the end of the first week "God saw all that he had made, and indeed, it was very good" (Gen. 1:31). The word used here for good also means beautiful. Theology is about the good and the beautiful in the work of God, in human life. For that reason theology cannot overlook that which breaks the beauty of this world and strangles the expression of human joy and happiness. If we approach human suffering, poverty, and injustice in solidarity with those who experience it, it is because the word about God is always a word about life and happiness. It is language about the One whom the Bible calls "you who love the living" (Wisd. Sol. 11:26).

Between Babel and Pentecost

Genuine theological language requires sinking roots into what André Malraux called "the human condition." To do so, such speech must keep in mind the cultural diversity of humankind. A reflection on a biblical paradigm that is now part of the common heritage of humankind can offer us some insight.

Mythical accounts arise in order to account for fundamental but disputed matters. The passage in Genesis known as the tower of Babel seeks to explain something that is lost in the obscurity of time, namely, the variety of tongues spoken by the human race. This narrative, generally read as a punishment by God for what is assumed to be a Promethean effort, has struck the imagination of the Western world over the centuries. The punishment meted out to those who wanted to "make a name for themselves" (Gen. 11:4) by building a tower that could reach up to the sky is said to have done away with an original single language (Gen. 11:1); those who were involved in the pretentious (Gen. 11:8–9) building project were struck with bewilderment and could no longer understand each other.

Such is the most common interpretation, the one prevailing in the popular imagination of the West. Nevertheless, the matter is worth reconsidering in relation to the topic that interests us, namely, the task of theology.

Dante and the Vernacular Languages

At different points in his work, Dante Alighieri alludes to the question of the vernacular languages which in his time were beginning to break away from Latin. He finally takes up the topic in a curious, unfinished treatise written in Latin, *De Vulgari Eloquentia* (Vernacular eloquence).

As a medieval man, Dante accepts the historicity of the tower of Babel story. He regrets the loss of humankind's protolanguage and regards the diversity of languages as the result of a divine punishment. To this point we find nothing especially remarkable; Dante seems to accept at face value the prevailing interpretation of the Genesis text in his time. The fact is, however, that ultimately he introduces substantial changes in it.

He does not hide his intention. The opening lines in his book speak of the vacuum that he is seeking to fill. "No one before us," he says, "had treated the doctrine of the vernacular tongue." That is the point. The vernacular language is the one "we learn" he says, "without any rule, imitating our wet nurse." He regards it as the one best fitted for expressing feelings of joy and love. The vernacular can be given no higher praise.

Dante says that the Babel episode is "worth recalling." What does he mean? Reading his treatise, one has the impression that he says this not so much because it reminds us of an exemplary chastisement to human audacity but because it opens the way to the vernacular languages. Babel thus becomes something of a *fe-*

lix culpa, a "happy fault" to which we owe the existence and the wealth of different languages, enabling us to express ourselves poetically. Punishment becomes reward, curse becomes blessing.

All of this does not mean that there is no yearning for a universal language in Dante. For him, however, that does not mean returning to the past; such yearning is toward the future and is aimed at overcoming the linguistic conditions arising at Babel. The *Divine Comedy,* for example, testifies to that yearning and search.

Curse or Blessing?

Dante's questioning interpretation of the Genesis text was not the only assault on the ordinary understanding of this passage, but it is certainly one of the most significant. His contribution was to raise doubts about the idea that diversity of language was purely and simply punishment from God.

Contemporary archaeological and historic research on the region of Mesopotamia has proved that in antiquity there were many cities built around very high towers. This has led some researchers to say that the first reference to the actual history of humankind that we find in the book of Genesis is precisely the tower of Babel account.

Such facts surely served as ingredients for the author or authors of the account. Moreover, the history of the Jewish people and a careful reading of other texts in the Bible sharpen the picture of the motivations for this story. On a number of occasions, for example, the Jews saw their territory occupied by the great empires of the region, and they were put into forced labor by the political leaders of the enemy country.

Hence, many modern exegetes say that the text must be read as the fruit of the painful historical experience of a subjugated people. All these elements enter into a literary composition that thereby becomes a paradigm of the life of humankind and takes its place beyond its location at a particular place and time.

Unquestionably, we have here a rejection of the haughtiness of those building the city and the tower. But more than a Promethean enterprise of rivalry with God, it is a political attempt, totalitarian in nature, to dominate people. To the extent that it is such, it is indeed an offense against God. Hence, the single language is not, in the story we are examining, the expression of an idyllic unity of humankind, nor must it be an ideal yearned for; instead, it must be seen as the imposition of an empire. Such a language facilitates centralized power and the political yoke. As the experience of history demonstrates, the matter arises spontaneously in those who hold power in their hands or are close to it. This is the topic, as we all recall, of the letter that Nebrija sends to Queen Isabel to offer her his new and classic *Gramática castellana* (Spanish grammar). The terms are well known.

Observation of history has convinced him that "language has always gone hand in hand with empire." They grow and flourish together and together they fall. The scholar Nebrija argues on behalf of his work by rooting it in the situation in 1492. He regards his book as especially timely at the moment when the queen has "under her yoke many barbarian peoples and nations of far-off tongues" — peoples that he says must receive "the laws that the victor imposes on the vanquished." Nothing better for that purpose than to learn "our language" suggests Nebrija, something that those nations can do better and more rapidly now, thanks to the grammar that he is placing in his sovereign's hands.

Elsewhere, at another moment that is equally decisive, politically speaking, this view of language makes a reappearance. Within the tumult of the social movements and debates of the French Revolution, an effort is made to forge a single nation with a firm central power. The paradigm of the confusion of Babel is again recalled. The utopian thinkers of the sixteenth century had also invoked it, but at this point we are witnessing the actual erection of a modern state. The famous Abbé Gregory denounces what to his eyes appears to be a great contradiction: "with thirty dialects, we are like Babel with respect to language, whereas we stand at the forefront of the nations with regard to freedom."

The variety of languages is thus evidence of a very serious backwardness: that variety must be done away with if progress toward modernity is to be made. The fateful legacy of Babel must be eradicated. Regional languages must disappear; establishing a single language for all would seal national unity. The single language becomes an important political tool in a modern world then taking its first steps. It will contribute to the development of the totalitarian thrust of what Jürgen Habermas calls "instrumental reason."

Nebrija and Gregory (as well as many others we could easily mention) thus stand on the side of power. Matters look different to those who suffer the consequences of an imperial and even totalitarian will. Just as it is denounced in Dostoyevsky's always terrifying legend of the Grand Inquisitor which makes people believe that they enjoy freedom. That would be the message of the Genesis text and the reason for rejecting the fiction of a human community expressed in a single language so as not to impede the flow of orders coming from the central authority.

Against this background, the diversity of languages for oppressed peoples, far from being a punishment, helps protect their freedom. It prevents a totalitarian power from imposing itself with no resistance. If there is punishment, it is directed at the effort of some to impose, and not the different nations speaking their own languages. Well-known contemporary exegetes and theologians have pointed out that this biblical passage does not speak of punishment.

Those same scholars have also observed that in the Book of Genesis as a whole the diversity of peoples and languages is presented as a great treasure for humankind and as desired by God.

We are clearly dealing with a polysemic text. For our purposes it suffices to say that an interpretation being put forth today is not only one that can claim ancient intuitions and can be traced through the history of the reading of this account over the centuries, but that is also based on a rigorous contemporary approach to the text and its context. Moreover, the current appreciation of ethnic and cultural pluralism opens new possibilities for understanding this foundational myth about the diversity of languages.

All in Their Own Language

We are thus led to be reminded of one of the most significant developments for contemporary Christianity: Christian faith has not only begun to arise in the hearts of non-Western peoples and cultures, but it has grown and matured there.

In an influential article seeking to assess Vatican Council II, Karl Rahner said that from a theological standpoint, three great periods could be discerned in the history of the Church: first, the short time between Jesus and Paul of Tarsus, linked to the Jewish world; then, the period between Paul and the eve of Vatican II in the twentieth century, linked to the Western world. The third moment, which began with Vatican II, faces the major challenge of dealing with universality in diversity. Historians might dispute Rahner's periodization, but it is undeniably stimulating and even provocative.

Recognition of the (culturally and ethnically) other is a major demand of our time. Over untraveled paths and unforeseen shortcuts the experience of neglected and abused peoples is becoming fruitful for the two great dimensions of Christian life: mysticism and human solidarity. It is there that a discourse on God is sinking its roots, a discourse that is not merely a reflection of what is occurring in places where Christianity has existed for many centuries.

Forced to become acclimated in a different environment and to take nourishment from the sap that comes from other lands, theological language gives hardy fruits whose flavor is somewhat different from the one to which many were accustomed, but they are not thereby less tasty and nutritious. The demands of what is now called inculturation — a new term for something quite old — which was emphasized by John Paul II and the bishops meeting several years ago in Santo Domingo (1992), go further than adaptation. They call for a renewal of mental categories.

This effort encompasses many current efforts to speak of God. What Dante said of the vernacular languages is true for theological language rooted in a particular social and cultural world. As they express in a unique way the initial feelings of joy and love (that is why they are the proper language of poetry), likewise the paths taken today by the word about God based on particular experiences are best fitted for powerfully and authentically giving voice to delight and pain and to hope and love. Discourse on God is not real and challenging except in the diversity with which it is formulated.

In this apology for particularity, however, what space remains for universality? The first point to be made is that theological languages are converging approaches toward the mystery recognized and invoked in faith, the root of every word about God. However, although fundamental, it is not the only basis for unity and universality; such words also depend on the human density that theological language bears within itself.

"A provincial of this world" Peruvian novelist José María Arguedas calls himself at one point. The human universality toward which Arguedas moves, starting with the Peruvian Indian and mestizo, bears the mark of the suffering and hope, the anguish and gentleness of those who are sometimes regarded as human refuse. Far from limiting his perspective, this stamp gives it breadth and effective power. "In the sound of the *charango* and the *quena* I shall hear *everything*," he says as he finished his *¿Ultimo Diario?* His is the concrete universality which, as Hegel said, is expressed in the singular.

To the extent that language about God takes on the human condition with its doubts and certainties, generosity and self-seeking, insecurity and constancy, laughter and tears, it passes through the density of the social, of gender, of the ethnic, and of the cultural so as to reach the deepest dimensions of the human. "If language thus loaded with strange essences," said Arguedas perceptively, "enables us to see the deep human heart, if it communicates to us the story of its movement over the earth, universality may perhaps be a long time in coming; it will nevertheless come, however, for we know very well that humans owe their preeminence and their dominion to the fact that they are one and unique." That is why he used to say mischievously, "I am a provincial of this world."

We will not have a lively language about God without a lucid and fruitful relationship with the culture of a time and a place. At the same time, the various particular theologies must establish close communication with one another, because they are striving for a word about singular situations situated in an ever more interdependent world.

The episode of Pentecost, sometimes regarded as the paradigm of a universal language, illustrates this necessary communication out of diversity. It is not about speaking a single language, but about being able to understand one another. The story tells of persons who have come from different places and have heard the disciples of Jesus and understood them — three times, it says — in their own language (Acts 2:6, 8, 11). All are speaking their own language, but they understand one another. Hence Pentecost, far from being a paradigm of anti-Babel, signifies instead that each of the various ethnic groups present in Jerusalem is prized. There is only one reservation: the legitimate linguistic differences between them must not only not hinder mutual understanding but favor it.

Language about God takes its inspiration from the Christian message but also — and inseparably — in the manner in which it is made up of life. This depends on very specific historic circumstances. No theology is without its own accent in speaking of God, a flavor, a special taste, which is what the word "accent" also means. The differences in such speaking must be respected. It is not imposed uniformity that is required, but understanding in diversity.

The Narrator Narrated

With its starting point in the density of human life, a language about God anchored in a particular cultural world must be capable of narrating the experience of Jesus and of those who have accepted his witness.

The Bible is composed of a wide variety of narrations; it is more stories than a single story or history. These accounts speak of the great issues of human concern: the origin of time, the reason for all that exists, the life and death of human beings, and the relationship with nature. Through the accounts, God — or more specifically God's humanity, Jesus — becomes present to those who accept God in their lives. The word about God must therefore bear this narrative imprint. The famous line by Blaise Pascal contrasting "the God of Abraham, Isaac, Jacob, and Jesus Christ" with the "God of the philosophers" is precisely the opposition between the God of narration and the God of concept and abstraction.

To tell of Christian practice, inspired by trust in love and in faith, means exchanging experiences. Such interchange, as the ever-acute Walter Benjamin put it, is "the surest reality among things that are sure." That is what Jesus did.

A Flavorful Knowledge

In the early days of Christianity, theology was simply a meditation on the Bible aimed at enriching the believer's everyday life or Christian practice. Theological language took the form of wisdom, again in the biblical meaning of the word: a knowing that has not lost its connection with savor, a delicious knowledge. This speaking also meant enjoying.[20]

Contact with the Greco-Roman world, and especially with philosophy, launched theology along the path of discourse and argumentation where the background was metaphysical. This encounter with Greek reason, and today with contemporary critical reason, led, and leads, to theological reflection of significance. It also shows its limits and its gaps, however.

For that reason it is obvious in our own time that, without discounting the contribution that we have just noted, it is important to highlight the narrative dimension mentioned earlier. For a long time, the philosophical perspective led to an interpretation of the well-known line of John's Gospel "in the beginning was the Word" (1:1) in the sense of the Greek *logos,* that is, concept and human reason. The complexity of the term with its Hebrew substrate was accordingly pushed to one side. Beneath the word *logos* used by John is the Hebrew *dabar,* which means simultaneously word and event. It is the *dabar,* thus understood with its double meaning, that stands at the beginning. It is the word made human flesh.

An event must be told, spoken. The story heard gives rise to other tellings. "What we have heard—that we tell," says a psalm.

20. Throughout this passage, titled "Un saber con sabor" in the original Spanish, there is wordplay between *saber* ("to know," "knowledge") and *sabor* ("flavor," "taste"). –*Trans.*

The result is a chain of narrative, composed of both the memory of past events and the imprint of other new ones. A believing community is always a narrating community.

Let us take, by way of example, a text familiar to us, the parable that we customarily call "The Good Samaritan." Prompted by the question, "Who is my neighbor?" Jesus tells the story of two somewhat prominent individuals within the Jewish people (both connected to religious worship) who remain unmoved by the suffering of someone they did not know, perhaps for reasons of ritual purity. The third individual is a Samaritan, who therefore belongs to a people and a religion that were then held in contempt. The Samaritan approaches the injured man and becomes his neighbor. The passage concludes with a short and unequivocal statement from Jesus to the individual to whom he has told the story: "Go and do likewise" (see Luke 10:29–39).

The text does not offer us a definition of the category "neighbor" nor a speech on charity or human solidarity. We stand before a simple but compelling comparison that calls us to have the capacity to be moved in the presence of a person who is abused and suffering and to effectively act to help that person.

Let us look at another Gospel text. This time it is not a parable, but the story of something Jesus does. I have in mind what we hastily call "The Multiplication of the Loaves." The story speaks to us of sensitivity to people's hunger, or sharing, and of knowing how to do so with the little that is at hand. At the end of the passage, the twelve baskets set in the middle of the grass are a call to keep sharing. Indeed, from now on sharing what one has must be the sign of those who accept the story. Hence, it is likewise the criterion making it possible to be discerning about human behavior.

There is no argument here based on definitions and doctrinal boundary setting, but rather a deed of love expressed in the sharing of bread. Here also we find a challenge to continue to do so throughout history. The great biblical accounts as well as the one that tells us the story of the life and death of Jesus have a value — today we would call it performative — for those who come into contact with them.

Jesus was a storyteller. His stories give rise to others that one way or another speak of him and of his witness. Jesus is the narrator narrated. From that standpoint, Christianity is simply a saga of stories. Storytelling is the proper way of speaking about God; this is not simply a literary form, much less a pedagogical device, as we are inclined to say of the Gospel parables; it is the proper language for speaking about God. Parables belong to the very nature of the Gospel.

Narration incorporates the hearer within it. It tells an experience and makes it an experience of those who hear it. The characteristic feature of the story is invitation, not obligation; its terrain is freedom, not command. A theology that takes its stand in story, that knows how to narrate faith, will be a theology that is humble and backed up by personal commitment, a theology that offers and does not seek to impose, one that listens before speaking. Truth emerges from silence, said Simone Weil shortly before her death. This is also true of speaking about God.

A Hermeneutic of Hope

Theology, says Paul Ricoeur, emerges at the intersection between "a space of experience" and "a horizon of hope." In that space there occurs a personal contact with the witness of Jesus, a Galilean itinerant preacher, whom we know through the biblical story. That hope is expressed not in the repetition of that narration, but in its re-creation in the life of those who feel called by the experience of Jesus and his friends. Theology is truly a hermeneutic of hope, a hermeneutic that must be done and redone continually. In Scripture it is called "giving an account of hope" (1 Pet. 3:15).

The witness of Jesus is ever challenging and disturbing. He tells us that human life reaches its full meaning only in total and daily surrender. The fact that he is the reference point is not a fixation on the past, but rather a way of bringing him into the present, so much so that memory of him has been regarded as dangerous for a history that is dominated by selfishness and injustice.

To recall, for example, the life and death of a man of our own time like Archbishop Oscar Romero is to tell faithfully and creatively the life and death of Jesus in the present of Latin America. With the Master, he could say,"No one takes my life from me; I lay it down on my own" (John 10:18). We can find this supreme act of freedom in other stories, many of them simple and every-day, and thus having less public impact. They all challenge those who live isolated from the suffering of others, but they are like-wise invitations to a change of attitude. Such proposals leave it up to our freedom and inventiveness to find the ways and also — why not? — the motivations that each one of us would like to have, leading to the practice of human solidarity.

The point is not that there is no room for logical argument and systematic thought in theology, but rather that they must always draw nourishment from a faith that reveals its full meaning only in a living and life-giving story. Although the telling is itself already a way of interpreting, there is undoubtedly a moment for narrating and a time for presenting arguments.

Theology must protect the categories of story and memory if it wants to remain faithful to its sources and to play a role in liberat-ing human beings from whatever hinders them from having their dignity respected and developing all their potentialities.

Theology must protect the categories of the story and memory in order to remain faithful to its sources and to fulfill its liberating task with regard to whatever prevents human beings from living in dignity and developing all their possibilities. Poor people do this instinctively when through stories and legends, which the an-thropologists do well to heed, they pull together the great human and Christian themes and through them express their faith in the liberating God.

Conclusion

Allow me a few closing words. Putting down roots in the dense and complex human condition of our peoples, centering its ex-pression on our social and cultural universe, and finally, taking seriously the narrative dimension of the Christian faith are essen-tial characteristics of the theological language that is developing in Latin America today.

This language represents something of a break with the immediate past and a great deal of continuity with the authentically traditional perspective which goes back to the sources of revelation. In a way we might say that this theology, like much of contemporary Latin American literature, tries to give a visible, audible presence to the poor, to those we think of as insignificant, to the invisible Garabombos of our history, to use the expression of Manuel Scorza.[21] This is an important convergence and a call to great fruitfulness.

The Greeks described as theologians the poets, like Homer and Hesiod (and also the mythical figure of Orpheus), who composed theogonies, mythological explanations of the origins of humanity. Plato himself was considered a theologian by the neoplatonists and the first Christian writers. Christian tradition draws the word "theology" from the Hellenic world, but keeps it in the dual context of its own origins and the present. The stories recalled a few moments ago are used to bring near and make real what would otherwise seem remote, imprisoned in the past. But the Greeks had the right idea: only poetic language, made of silence and words, is capable of making present those who sometimes seem absent to us. Juan de la Cruz, who speaks of "the silent melody" and of "resonant solitude," and Teresa of Avila with her dwellings and absences, each in their own way show us that meaningful possibility.[22]

Different biblical stories show us that the appropriate response to a friend's suffering is to keep silence, walking with them before speaking to them. Guamán Poma spoke of his thirty years of invisibility and silence in the midst of the Indians, his brothers. Without that prior condition, theological language may be only an arid, impersonal attitude, deserving the admonition of Job to the theologians who tried to teach him: "I have heard many such things; miserable comforters are you all. Have windy words no limit?" (Job 16:2–3). We don't want the poor of this continent to

---

21. *Historia de Garabombo, el invisible* (Barcelona: Planeta, 1972).
22. Theologian David Tracy says that we must "somehow learn, in the absent presence of God, to be still and know that God is God" ("El retorno de Dios en la teología contemporánea," *Concilium* 256 [December 1994]: 73).

reproach us for a way of talking that does not first hear and share their suffering, that does not feel the suffering of others.

For me, to do theology is to write a love letter to the God in whom I believe, to the people to whom I belong, and to the Church of which I am a part. It is a love that recognizes perplexity, even disgust, but that above all brings deep joy.

I have not mentioned, because it is so obvious, that personally I have much to learn from the Academia de la Lengua in whose ranks you have so kindly included me. But I do want to say before ending this long dissertation that my field, that of theology, also has much to learn from you. Thank you for your presence and your welcome.

— *Translated by James B. Nickoloff and Margaret Wilde*

Index

rich countries: and development,
121; and justice, 7; lifestyle of,
55–56
Rivas, María Agustina, 145–46
Romero, Oscar, 204–5

Salvatierra, Angel, 114–15
Santo Domingo meeting 1992:
document produced by, 113–
23; on human rights, 120–22;
preparations for, 102–15; request
for forgiveness of the oppressed,
119; and theology, 177; three
pastoral lines of, 114–18, 183–85
Saulchoir School, The (Chenu), 170
Second Vatican Council. *See*
Vatican II
signs of the times, 4–6, 11, 63, 120,
148–50
silence, 206–7
sin, poverty rooted in, 154–55
slave trade, the, 102
Social Action, Department of,
75–76
socialism, collapse of, 45–46, 48–50
social sciences, influence of, 125,
128–31
solidarity: with poor, 44, 92–100,
122–23, 153–55; in search for
justice, 151–52; with workers,
26–30
Sollicitudo Rei Socialis, encyclical
(John Paul II), 40, 44–45
storytelling, 204
Suenens, Leo Josef, 64
suffering: of the innocent, 188–94;
vs. sadness, 144, 161
Summa Theologica (Aquinas), 170

theocentrism, 143, 148, 165–68
theology: ecclesial function of,
169–86; and evangelization,
177–79; and hope, 204; of the
human person, 13–17; in *Laborem
Exercens,* 4–11; as language, 174,

178–79, 186–207; of liberation,
47–48, 81–82, 91–92, 107–
8, 127–28, 177–80; narrative
in, 202–5; poetry in, 144–45,
191–93, 199–201; and poverty,
127–34; role of reflection in, 171–
75; and social science, 128–31;
spirituality in, 135, 167–68, 175;
studying vs. doing, 169–72
"Theology" (Congar), 170
Todas las sangres (Arguedas), 191
totalitarianism, 45–47
Tupac Amaru II, 108

¿Ultimo Diario? (Arguedas), 200
U.S. Department of State, 49

Valdivieso, Antonio, 104
Valencia, Gerardo, 81
Vallejo, César, 192–93
Vatican II: and ecumenical dialogue,
65–66; and identity of Church,
60–61; misinterpretations of, 147;
modern world as theme, 63–65;
as new phase in history, 199;
and option for the poor, 24–26,
62–70; and signs of the times, 4
verification: of faithfulness to
Christ, 28–33; historical, 10–11
violence, 87–88, 126, 137–38, 179
Vulgari Eloquentia, De (Alighieri), 195

women, condition of, 119–20, 132
work, human: as alienated, 15–16;
Christ and, 12, 14–19; freedom
of, 54; in Genesis, 13–14, 16–17,
34–35; and God's work, 11–12,
17, 19; gospel of, 3–38; punitive
concept of, 16–17; respect for,
10–11, 30–31; spirituality of,
33–36
World War II, tensions following,
46–48

Yucay, document of, 104